Visitation
The Certainty of Alien Activity

Alternatives
Life Options for Today

Visitation

The Certainty of Alien Activity

PETER HOUGH

LONDON
HOUSE

First published in Great Britain in 1999 by
LONDON HOUSE
114 New Cavendish Street
London W1M 7FD

A catalogue record for this book is available
from the British Library

ISBN 1 902809 09 2

Edited and designed by DAG Publications Ltd, London.
Printed and bound by Biddles Limited,
Guildford, Surrey.

Contents

Introduction

A few days before starting this book, I went to a party held in an old rambling vicarage, just a short walk from where I live. The rooms were gaily decorated and filled with people in fancy dress. There was much laughter and dancing, clinking of glasses and acres of food. A huge pan of chilli con carne sat bubbling on the hob, and it was the best I have ever tasted. Praise indeed from someone who prides himself on producing a mean and hot chilli!

My host was wearing a dirty raincoat and posing as a flasher, to the hilarity of one and all. He is the manager of a local bookshop which stocks several of my titles. Word soon spread that I was a writer and investigator of the 'unexplained'. I was collared by first one, and then another of the guests eager to know more, and keen to impress upon me their own belief, or otherwise, in the Unknown.

Some had their own experiences to tell. One man was a believer in almost everything, from the face on Mars to back-engineered UFOs. His blind faith brought on a succession of yawns, which I did my best to hide.

The uncritical believer is every bit as bad as the debunker. Each eye-balls the other across the divide, two faces of the same coin. Their views are polarised, without objectivity or imagination, leaving no room for reasoned argument. The protagonists snipe at one another above the heads of those of us who occupy the middle ground, lacking any desire to see the fallacies of their own arguments or to examine the evidence in a fair-handed way.

There is no doubt that the UFO phenomenon represents something 'real' and under intelligent control. Beyond that nothing is certain.

At one point during the evening, I fell into conversation with a pleasant enough chap wearing a dinner suit. He was a survivor of the *Titanic*, and, in this world, worked as a physicist for British Nuclear

Fuels. Overhearing a previous conversation, Dr Penguin said some-what emphatically, 'There are no extraterrestrials visiting the Earth because it is impossible to build a spacecraft that can travel the vast distances between stars.'

The good doctor hardly flinched as I nodded in agreement. Although I would not rule it out altogether, I explained, it was also *my* belief that beings were not arriving here from outer space. However, I added that while I did not believe in extraterrestrials, I did accept aliens.

My friend's brow wrinkled up at this, leaving him bemused for a moment. When I began to talk of quantum mechanics and the theory that we might exist in a *multi*-universe – an infinite number of alter-native realities that could interact with our own – he smiled, adding smugly: 'I know several quantum physicists. And none of them can agree on this matter!'

With a curt wave of his hand, he dismissed my argument. It made more sense to me that the forces behind the UFO phenomenon originated in another dimension than from a different planet. Now he was back on safer ground ... or so he thought.

'If the aliens are here,' Dr Penguin said, puffing out his chest, 'why haven't they landed on the White House lawn?'

It was my turn to smile. How often had I been asked this very same question by countless other supposedly intelligent people?

'Your question is redundant,' I told him, 'and entirely without relevance.' He looked stunned.

'Don't you see?' I asked. 'You are *anthropomorphising* the phenomenon, attributing human logic, wishes and needs to an "alien" intelligence, which, by its very definition, would have a wholly different agenda, if any at all.'

This seemed to be beyond my scientist friend's comprehension. It brought home to me once again the ignorance shown by sceptics of the utter complexities of the UFO phenomenon. They and the media live in a two-dimensional world of black and white. UFOs and aliens either represent extraterrestrial visitations, or it is all down to misperception, hallucination, wish fulfilment and fraud. They are blind to the subtle shades of grey in between. Indeed, it seems that some sceptics deliberately ignore them. It is so much easier to argue a case against the reality of aliens if it is assumed they are supposedly from across the galaxy. After all, the phenomenon exhibits the trappings of extraterrestrials, so why should we not take it at face value?

When a man knocks on the door and says he wants to read your meter, do you automatically assume he is from the power company or insist on identification?

Dr Penguin made one last parting shot before he left me to refill his glass.

'Where is the *proof* that aliens are here?' he asked. *'What do they want?'*

'Proof' is a transient concept. What serves as proof for one man is inadequate for another. Millions believe that Christ could turn water into wine and rose from the dead. Others question his very existence.

What this book sets out to do is provide sufficient evidence of alien activity to make any fair-minded person realise that *something* real and concrete is going on, that UFO experiences and encounters represent an objective intelligence. I will also attempt to slip behind the smoke screen of the meter man to speculate on the true nature and origin of the 'aliens.' As to why 'they' are *here, and what do 'they' want*, I have some ideas on that, too.

Please read this book with an open mind. Afterwards, the world may not seem to be the place you thought it was ...

One final word. Names that initially appear in inverted commas denote that the witnesses' names have been changed to protect their privacy.

1

Exposing the Big Lie

The public are the victim of a Big Lie. Most people believe that alien activity began in 1947 with the crash of a UFO in New Mexico and pilot Kenneth Arnold's historic sighting of nine objects which 'flew like a saucer would if you skipped it across water.' A few years ago, authors and publishers conspired to produce shelves of books 'celebrating fifty years of UFOs', reinforcing the myth. They popularised the misconception that after World War Two we suddenly attracted the attentions of extraterrestrials, *when in fact the UFO phenomenon has been with us in various guises since written records began*.

So who masterminded the Big Lie, and what was its purpose? Was it the ufologists, the media or the intelligence community? *I believe it was the aliens themselves*, because that is the second part of the Big Lie. The forces behind the phenomenon have fostered a belief in visiting extraterrestrials.

It is easy to see why it was so readily embraced in the immediate years following the war. After it ceased, there was much talk about turning science fiction into science fact with the development of spacecraft which could fly to other worlds. Nineteen forty-seven was only ten years before the first satellite, Sputnik 1, was put into orbit and just fourteen years prior to the first manned spaceship being successfully launched in 1961. More than at any previous time, travel between the stars seemed a distinct possibility. If it was on the cards for us, it seemed plausible that advanced beings from other planets had already mastered space travel.

So if alien activity has been with us since the dawn of mankind, why was it suddenly perceived as extraterrestrial? The answer is, as I will demonstrate, because it *wanted* to be interpreted that way. That was the lie within the lie. There are no extraterrestrials, but there are aliens ...

Alien Activity In The Past

Alien activity in the distant past has been well documented. There should be no doubt that what we regard today as the UFO phenomenon was as active then as it is now. Sanskrit texts originally written ten thousand years ago vividly and unambiguously describe flying machines used by an elitist group of humans and beings from other worlds. Known as 'vimanas', these aerial craft were constructed of a light-weight alloy, powered by a 'mercury engine' and directed by thought. The *Samarangana Sutradhara* states that 'by means of these machines, human beings can fly in the air and heavenly beings can come down to Earth'.

Was the technology passed down to humans by aliens? Ironically, a similar claim is made today that extraterrestrials are trading their technology with the American government in exchange for permission to abduct a quota of human beings for genetic experimentation. Futuristic aircraft like the Stealth bomber which has radar invisibility are supposedly the fruits of this co-operation.

During the Japanese Jomon Era, which ended around 3000 BC, the making of earthen statues was an important artistic activity. The first statues were small, straightforward representations of human beings, but then the dimensions became much larger and the designs changed drastically. They portrayed beings with big chests, bowed legs, very short arms and large heads covered completely by helmets.

Archaeologists proposed that these were mourning masks worn at funerals. However, statues found in the Tohoku region appear to show sun-glasses – huge eyes with an insect-like horizontal slit. One dated 4300 BC excavated in the Iwate prefecture has a round opening at the base of the nose covered with what appears to be a perforated plate. A modern interpretation of these images would be an alien being wearing a one-piece space suit with a helmet, complete with goggles and breathing filter.

This is interesting in view of the fact that ancient Japanese records contain a UFO sighting dated October 27, 1180, where an unusual luminous object described as an 'earthenware vessel' flew from a mountain in the Kii province at midnight. After a while, the object changed course, leaving a luminous trail.

A collection of cylinder seals created by the Phoenicians between 400 and 300 BC reside in the British Museum. Five of these depict a winged disc, with 'divine beings' emerging from the objects on four of them. Dwarves are pictured in conjunction with the beings. Humans are shown in positions of adoration before the discs. In some scenes, animals are carried to the hovering objects, reminding us of modern animal mutilation cases associated with UFO sightings.

Proof that the ancients attained technologically advanced aerial flight is presented in the form of the Piri Re'is map discovered in 1929 during conversion work at the Palace of Topkapi in Istanbul. Dated 1513, it was originally in the possession of Admiral Piri Re'is and shows South America, part of Africa and an area of coastline now buried beneath the Antarctic. Because of the latter, it seems reasonable to assume that the map is a copy of a much older chart drawn around six thousand years ago. At that time, Queen Maud Land and its neighbouring regions passed through an ice-free period. Whoever, or whatever, had drawn the original map could only have done it from orbit around the Earth. Today the coastline is buried under a mile of ice.

In the 1960s and 1970s, a number of best-selling books were published which supposedly proved that mankind was influenced by aliens in biblical times. Many of the arguments were flawed. In particular, Swiss author Erich von Danekin came in for some well deserved criticism. The topic has suffered a renaissance in recent years and von Danekin's books are back in print. Despite its shortcomings, there is some compelling evidence for the 'ancient astronaut' theory.

The Spaceships Of Ezekiel

Many episodes in the Old Testament can be interpreted as events where aliens meddled with the genetic and cultural evolution of early humans. This was proposed as early as 1959 by the Russian ethnologist M. M. Agrest. One of the staple passages from the Bible which proponents of the theory have often quoted is from Ezekiel I, where the prophet describes a 'vision' while standing on the banks of the River Chebar and his subsequent abduction:

> As I looked, behold, a stormy wind came out of the north,
> and a great cloud, with brightness round about it, and fire

flashing forth continually, and in the midst of the fire, as it were gleaming bronze. And from the midst of it came the likeness of four living creatures.

And this was their appearance: They had the form of men, but each had four faces, and each of them had four wings. Their legs were straight, and the soles of their feet were like the sole of a calf's foot; and they sparkled like burnished bronze. Under their wings on their four sides they had human hands. And the four had their faces and their wings thus: their wings touched one another; they went every one straight forward, without turning as they went.

As for the likeness of their faces, each had the face of a man in front, the four had the face of a lion on the right side, the four had the face of an ox on the left side, and the four had the face of an eagle on the back. And their wings were spread out above; each creature had two wings, each of which touched the wing of another, while two covered their bodies.

In the midst of the living creatures there was something that looked like burning coals of fire, like torches moving to and fro; and the fire was bright, and out of the fire went forth lightening. And the living creatures darted to and fro, like a flash of lightening.

Now as I looked at the living creatures, I saw a wheel upon the earth beside the living creatures, one for each of the four of them. As for the appearance of the wheels and their construction: their appearance was like the gleaming of a chrysolite; and the four had the same likeness, their construction being as it were a wheel within a wheel. When they went, they went in any of their four directions without turning as they went. The four wheels had rims and they had spokes; and their rims were full of eyes around about. And when the living creatures went, the wheels were beside them; and when the living creatures rose from the earth, the wheels rose.

Over the heads of the living creatures there was the likeness of a firmament, shining like crystal, spread out above their heads. And under the firmament their wings were stretched out straight, one toward another; and each creature had two wings covering its body. And when they went, I heard the sound of their wings like the sound of many waters, like the thunder of the Almighty, a sound of tumult like the sound of a host; when they stood still, they let down their wings.

This is a powerful, enigmatic piece of descriptive prose: one can sense Ezekiel struggling to convey in words a vision which represented something totally outside his experience and understanding. What comes across more than anything is the utter complexity of the phenomenon witnessed by the prophet. However, modern-day proponents of the ancient astronaut theory have no doubts as to what Ezekiel saw – flying machines of alien origin. This interpretation was given a boost by NASA scientist Josef Blumrich.

Blumrich was chief of the systems layout branch at the Marshall Spaceflight Center, and worked on the Saturn rocket and the design of Skylab. He looked at Ezekiel's vision from the point of view of someone who had never seen a flying machine before, and examined the descriptive passages in close detail. Blumrich looked for meaning in Ezekiel's kaleidoscope of awesome images. In what some had interpreted as a waking dream, the NASA engineer saw the description of the arrival of alien hardware in the form of a sort of helicopter.

He developed his very technical thesis into a book called *The Spaceships of Ezekiel*. In it, he said, 'We should consider that Ezekiel first saw this vehicle at a distance of about 1,000 metres; at that moment the nuclear engine fired, probably with some white clouds of condensation.'

The rounded 'soles of the feet' was the same design that Blumrich and his NASA colleagues had used on plans which would allow a spacecraft to slide on landing. Blumrich commented at how unbird-like the wings of the creatures sounded, and saw them as the blades of helicopters. The four faces of the creatures, he said, reminded him of the images of animals our own pilots paint on the noses and fuselages of aircraft. More than anything, the twentieth century engineer was drawn by the prophet's repetitive and detailed description of the wheels, which Ezekiel said was 'a wheel within a wheel'. Blumrich wrote, 'No one has ever taken seriously the functional description which indicates that the wheels could move in any direction without being turned or steered.'

However, he *did* take it seriously, and in 1974 patented the Omnidirectional Wheel. From the biblical account, Blumrich reconstructed a humming-top-shaped spacecraft which accommodated four helicopter landing vehicles. All he needed was a nuclear powered engine to allow the vehicle to be built and tested.

Of course, there have been critics of Josef Blumrich's interpretation of Ezekiel's vision. Author Edward Ashpole pondered 'does this spaceship belong to Ezekiel or Blumrich?' I suspect that Blumrich was really on to something when he tried to dig beneath the metaphors of Ezekiel's account, but perhaps his enthusiasm ran away with him.

The Sirius Saga

One of the most convincing cases supporting alien activity in the ancient past involves the Dogon people of West Africa. Robert K. G. Temple read an essay published in 1954 by two eminent anthropologists, Marcel Giaule and Gemaine Dieterlen, which started him on a journey of discovery culminating in his book *The Sirius Mystery* originally published in 1976, and up-dated for a new 1998 edition.

The Dogon, whom Temple later grew to believe were derived from the ancient Egyptians, seemed to have a detailed knowledge of the Sirius star system. This had been prized for thousands of years, and was passed down through generations. They knew that Sirius 'A', the brightest star in the sky, had a much smaller companion, which was very 'heavy.' Verification for this can be found in the Pyramid Texts where Sirius is compared to Isis 'great with child', the clear implication being that the star is a dual entity. The Dogons also knew that Sirius 'B' took fifty years to orbit its larger companion, even though the smaller star was only visible through the most powerful telescopes.

In 1844, astronomer Johann Friedrich Bessel speculated that Sirius was a binary star system, but this was not confirmed until 1862 by another astronomer, Alvin Clark. Not until over half a century later was it discovered that one of the duo possessed eccentric properties that made it unusually heavy. Although only three times the radius of the Earth, Sirius 'B' had a mass just a little less than our sun. With that came the finding of the first 'white dwarf', a star that has collapsed in on itself until it is only a hundredth of its former size.

Temple found that the Dogon people had a wide range of astronomical knowledge, which was handed down over thousands of years. They knew that planets moved in elliptical orbits and referred to the moon as 'dry and dead, like dry, dead blood'. The Dogons appreciated that the Earth revolved on its axis, that Saturn had rings and were knowledgeable of four of Jupiter's major moons. Temple discovered an entire mythology which matched late twentieth century scientific knowledge. Where had it come from?

According to tradition, their ancestors learned everything from an amphibious race of beings called the 'Nommos', who arrived from the Sirius star system. This is how the Dogon described the arrival of the Nommos 'ark':

> The ark landed and displaced a pile of dust raised by the whirlwind it caused. The violence of the impact roughened the ground. He is like a flame that went out when he touched the earth.

After the craft landed, it moved into a hollow which filled with water, whereupon the aliens emerged. A description of the Nommos is given by a Babylonian historian called Berossus, who lived at the time of Alexander the Great, 356–323 BC:

> The whole body of the animal was like that of a fish, and had under a fish's head another head, and also feet below, similar to those of a man, subjoined to the fish's tail. His voice too, and language, were articulate and human; and a representation of him is preserved even to this day ... When the sun set, it was the custom of this Being to plunge again into the sea, and abide all night in the deep; for he was amphibious.

The connection with the global mythology of mermen and mermaids is obvious. Robert Temple found representations of the Nommos all over the Middle East in the form of stone carvings and drawings featuring beings adorned with fish tails. One of them was a Babylonian semi-demon called Oannes, who was said to have founded the first human civilisations on Earth. In support of this, Temple notes how the Sumerian culture seems to have sprung from nowhere, and how 3,400 years BC the Egyptians passed quickly from a Neolithic culture to one exemplified by writing and major building construction.

Critics of the Sirius saga suggested that twentieth century missionaries gave the Dogon their astronomical knowledge. But this is absurd and would mean the Dogon were lying when they said the knowledge had been passed down through thousands of years. Temple proved this could not be the case.

One weakness in the story was the Dogon's insistence that there was a third star, Sirius 'C'. This was supposedly observed by astronomers in 1920, 1926, 1928 and 1929. Since then others have looked for it, but found no trace. That was the position in 1976 when Robert Temple first published his book. Then in 1995 French astronomers Daniel Benest and J. L. Duvent released the results of their observations of the Sirius star system. They had detected a perturbation which could only have one cause – the presence of a small red dwarf star. Sirius 'C' had been found ...

This is evidence indeed of alien activity thousands of years before Christ. It also demonstrates that since man's inception on this planet, other-world beings have directed his evolution, moulded his culture and, as we shall see, manipulated his thoughts and abused his freedom. These beings are also responsible for the Big Lie.

The Nommos claimed they were extraterrestrials from Sirius. That cannot be true. The Sirius system does not offer the sort of stable conditions for an Earth-type planet to evolve in order to promote intelligent life. Throughout the history of alien activity, the beings have been at pains to convince us they are extraterrestrials, but this is nothing but a red herring to divert our attention from the Truth.

Little Green Men

When former police officer 'Philip Spencer' set off across Ilkley Moor in the early morning of December 1, 1987, he did not expect to be confronted by a being from another world. Nor could he have understood the ramifications of the experience.

Spencer was walking from the Yorkshire town of Ilkley to the village of East Morton on the far side of the moor. He set off at around 7.10 am and took with him his camera to photograph Ilkley from the hills above as the sun was rising. The young man never took those pictures.

He wound his way around the back of the old White Wells building on the edge of the moor, took a path along a gully, then climbed up onto the hills. The next event he remembered was seeing 'a green creature' standing in a large hollow just off the footpath. The being fled further into the hollow, stopped, turned, and made a dismissive motion with its right hand. Spencer brought up his camera and took one shot before it turned and disappeared behind an outcrop. He ran after the creature and was just in time to see a metallic disc-shaped object lift off and quickly disappear into low cloud.

It subsequently emerged that almost two hours were 'missing' from Spencer's conscious recollection of that morning. Clinical psychologist Jim Singleton hypnotised the young man and took him back to 're-live' the experience. It emerged that Spencer was abducted by the being earlier in the walk, and then placed back on the moor with no conscious recollection. He was therefore surprised at seeing the creature that had just released him, and took the photograph. This case is treated in great depth in my book *The Truth About Alien Abductions*, written with Dr Moyshe Kalman.

What is relevant is the context of the experience mythologically, historically and contemporarily. When I asked Mrs Spencer to comment on the photograph her husband had taken, she said, 'Well, it looks like a demon, doesn't it?' The image of the 137 centimetre-high figure is blurred due to camera shake, but it is clear enough to justify Mrs Spencer's observation.

Philip Spencer gave a full description of the 'green creature' under hypnosis, stating: 'It's quite small. He's got big pointed ears; it's got big eyes. They're quite dark. He hasn't got a nose. He's only got a little mouth. And his hands are enormous. And his arms are long. He's got funny feet. They're like a V-shape, like two big toes ...'

Spencer is describing cloven hoofs. What is a pagan god doing travelling in a 'spaceship'? There is a further twist in the tale. During my investigation of the case, I discovered that Spencer's experience was only the latest in a long line of mysterious incidents that had occurred on Ilkley Moor. There are certain places that seem to be window areas where strange phenomena are concentrated. Are these locations *portals between different worlds*?

An incident which I found relevant involved a local man one hundred and seventy two years earlier. The White Wells building is constructed around a natural spring, and was bequeathed for bathing to the people of Ilkley at the beginning of the nineteenth century. One morning in 1815 William Butterfield, the bathman in charge of opening the premises, arrived as usual and placed his key in the lock. He was astonished when it spun round of its own accord, but even more taken aback when looking inside.

Jumping in and out of the water 'were a lot of little creatures dressed in green, none more than eighteen inches high, [46 centimetres] making a chatter and a jabber'. The 'creatures' bounded towards him 'like squirrels. Then the whole tribe went, helter-skelter, toppling and tumbling, heads over heels.' Butterfield watched as they disappeared up the gully behind the building – the same route which Philip Spencer was to take all those years later.

The story is more than folklore. It was written down by another man in the town after he interviewed the witness. William Butterworth's experience demonstrates that the stories of elves, fairies and gnomes were as real in their day as are contemporary encounters with so-called extraterrestrials. There are many parallels between the two which show they are strands of the same weave. Philip Spencer was apparently abducted by a cloven hoofed extraterrestrial, but human beings have been taken away long before the modern space age – by fairies.

UFO abductees, as we will see later in the book, are taken for examination and experimentation after which, as in Spencer's case, they are often given a tour of the 'spacecraft', as if to reinforce the lie. As we saw with the Ilkley case, this usually lasts for just a few hours or less. In the centuries before the industrial revolution, humans also reported abduction by small beings to fairy land, where they would stay for several years before being returned. In Reginald Scot's *The Discovery of Witchcraft* published in 1665 the following passage appears:

And many have been taken away by the said spirits, for a fortnight or month together, being carried with them in chariots through the air, over hills and dales, rocks and precipices, till at last they have been found lying in some meadow or mountain, bereaved of their senses.

An Irish man who was abducted for seven years described a land of fine estates and grand houses whilst another told of 'the most splendid town that was ever seen'. The Little People lived in opulence in a world inaccessible to human beings, unless the fairies chose to take them there.

Access to this world was through secret entrances in the hills and earth mounds where the fairies were said to live. However, the inside bore no relationship to the outside, opening out into huge vistas. Are modern-day, dome-shaped UFOs analogous to these magical earth mounds? Some maintain that fairies reside in large toadstools, which are reminiscent of the saucer-shaped objects occupied by alien beings. In his book *The Science of Fairy Tales*, Edwin Hartland narrates a traditional story from Denmark. When he describes the fairy knoll, Hartland writes, 'The hillock was standing, as is usual on such occasions, on red pillars.'

Not all fairy abductions were successful. At the beginning of the twentieth century, anthropologist Evans Wentz was told the following by the Reverend J. M. Spicer, of Malew on the Isle of Man:

The belief in fairies is quite a living thing here yet. For example, old Mrs K., about a year ago, told me that on one occasion, when her daughter had been in Castletown during the day, she went out to the road at nightfall to see if her daughter was yet in sight, whereupon a whole crowd of fairies suddenly surrounded her, and began taking her off toward South Barrule Mountain; and, she added, 'I couldn't get away from *them* until I had called my son.'

This reminds us of the classic abduction case of Betty and Barney Hill, who were ambushed by a crowd of UFO entities on September 19, 1961, while travelling through New England in the USA. The beings carried them off to their 'spaceship' for experimental purposes.

'Fairy lights' were often reported in conjunction with the Little People, or Gentry, to use an Irish term. At the time of the Malew report, two sisters who lived near the fairy fort of Crillaun in Ireland saw lights on several occasions during calm nights. One reported red, green, blue and yellow lights while the other described white lights flying in formation on a course that took them across to another fort.

In his *Treatise of Spirits* published in 1705, John Beaumont described his encounters and contacts with the fairies. On one occasion, he asked them who they were. He received the reply 'they were an order of creatures superior to mankind, and could influence our thoughts, and that their habitation was in the air'.

A fascinating account of a Close Encounter of the Third Kind (CE3) survives in an official police report made in 1790. Inspector Liabeuf, a doctor, the mayors of two nearby towns and three other officials were amongst those who witnessed the affair on June 12, near Alencon, France. Here is an excerpt from the report:

At 5 am, several farmers caught sight of an enormous globe, which seemed surrounded with flames. First they thought it was perhaps a balloon that had caught fire, but the great velocity and the whistling sound which came from the body intrigued them.

The globe slowed down, made some oscillations and precipitated itself towards the top of a hill. The heat which emanated from it was so intense that soon the grass and small trees started burning.

The sphere, which would have been large enough to contain a carriage, had not suffered from the flight. It excited so much curiosity that people came from all parts to see it. Then all of a sudden a kind of door opened and a person like us came out of it, but this person was dressed in a strange way, wearing a tight fitting suit and, seeing that crowd, said some words which were not understood and fled into the wood. Instinctively, the peasants stepped back in fear, and this saved them because soon after that the sphere exploded in silence, throwing pieces everywhere, and these pieces burned until they were reduced to powder.

Searches were initiated to find the mysterious man, but he seemed to have dissolved.

What gives this case the stamp of authenticity is the silent explosion of the object. There are many contemporary accounts where witnesses describe how the UFO 'silently' exploded. It is interesting that the being fled into the wood, the natural habitat of the elves and fairies, or *fees* as they were called in Brittany.

In Mexico, the source of many contemporary UFO sightings, there has long been an ancient tradition of belief in small black beings called *ikals*, a Mayan word meaning 'spirit'. Anthropologist Brian Stross learned of many incidents involving the metre-tall entities after talking to the Tzeltal Indians. Stross was told that in 1947 there was a flurry of incidents. In some of them, the Indians tried to attack the *ikals* with their machetes. During one encounter a tribesman was approached by a spherical object. He struck at it with his machete and it disintegrated, leaving an ash-like substance.

Stross discovered that the beings were believed to be from another world. Some were reported having a rocket-like apparatus attached to their backs, with which they were able to carry off people. Veteran ufologist Gordon Creighton, a linguistics expert, made a study of Indian folklore whilst living in South America as a British Diplomat. He uncovered further details regarding the *ikals*, reporting that they were particularly partial to abducting human women, who were then adapted for cross breeding.

The Long And The Short And The Tall

What do the Little People look like? A whole menagerie of beings have been reported down the centuries, from aggressive, hairy trolls and tiny entities just a few inches high with gossamer wings to little people mimicking the dress and culture of human beings. It may surprise new students to the subject, but until the mid-1980s UFO entities similarly varied in appearance. Indeed, at that time there was an almost total lack of consistency in descriptions.

UFO occupants were variously described as tall, small, thin, fat, human-like, grotesque, saintly, covered in fur, hairless, with long arms, short arms, hands, claws, large heads, headless, friendly, menacing, indifferent, capable of levitating, passing through solid objects and vanishing – in an instant!

On September 3, 1976, at 9 pm, two women, one aged eighteen and the other sixty-three, were walking past waste land in the mining village of Fencehouses, County Durham, when a strange object sitting atop a mound of earth made them stop. It was about 152 centimetres long, 106 centimetres high, oval shaped with an orange dome, the entire object resting on runners like those of a sleigh.

Drawing closer, all exterior sound diminished as they entered an altered state of consciousness. People confronted by fairies often described how they were 'enchanted', captivated by a magical spell. Then the women were startled by the sudden appearance of two strange beings half a metre tall, with long, white hair parted in the middle, which framed eyes much larger than those of a human. The aliens entered the UFO. It then took off making a humming sound, leaving the women quaking with fear.

A truly bizarre incident involving goblin-like entities happened in 1955 on a farm near Hopkinsville, Kentucky. On the night of August 21, Billy Ray Taylor went out to the well on the Sutton Farm when he saw a huge shining object land in a nearby river bed. He went back indoors and told the Suttons, but they just laughed. Less than an hour later, one of their dogs began barking out in the yard. Billy and his friend Lucky Sutton went to investigate – and were astounded to see a strange figure walking towards them with its arms in the air, as if in surrender.

The being was about a metre tall with a bald, egg-shaped head, and yellow eyes the size of saucers. Between elephant-like ears stretched a gash of a mouth. It had short, thin legs and long arms that finished in claws. The creature glowed as if illuminated from the inside.

The young men fired at the being with a shotgun and a .22 rifle. There was a sound like shooting into a metal bucket. Despite being just six metres away, the visitor somersaulted backwards ... and scurried away, evidently uninjured.

This was the beginning of several hours' terror. Other identical creatures converged on the farm from all directions. They stared through the windows at the occupants, and only withdrew when they were fired at or an outside light was switched on. Despite hitting several of the creatures, they always scurried away without a mark. Billy went outside and a hand reached down from the roof and ruffled his hair. He was dragged back inside. Lucky pumped several shots into the being, which fell unharmed from the roof. Another entity in the branches of a maple tree floated down to the ground after being shot, then ran away.

After four hours of terror, the family and their friend made a run for it, piling into two cars, heading for the police station. Police officers returned with them, but despite evidence of gun fire there was no trace of the strange object or the entities. The officers left the family in the early hours of the morning – when the beings reappeared. They left for good at sunrise. Despite the terror generated by the visitors, during the whole time of the 'siege', the beings made no moves to injure the farm people.

South America in particular has generated a large number of reports featuring UFO entities that resembled elves and gnomes. A saucer-shaped object was seen flying over Pernambuco in Brazil on October 26, 1965. At about noon, Jose Camilho, a car mechanic with a good reputation, was passing along a road through a belt of scrub land when he noticed two small people sitting like children on the stump of a fallen banana tree.

When he approached, they jumped to their feet. Camilho saw they were less than a metre tall, with shrivelled, brown faces, white hair, round, disproportionally large heads, and slitted oriental eyes. One had a sparse beard and wore a dark peaked cap. Camilho noted that one of them carried a rod-shaped object and 'looked so astonished it seemed his eyes would leap from their sockets'. The small being indicated to the Brazilian it was a weapon of some sort.

The other entity reacted more calmly and wore a shirt, trousers and footwear similar to tennis shoes. Around his waist was a luminous belt featuring an array of bright flashing lights. Between the entities stood a cylinder about the same height as them. The little man wearing the belt staggered off with it, comically colliding with his nervous companion, almost falling to the ground. Camilho returned home bewildered.

I investigated a case in 1976 which involved an elf-like entity. Mrs Mary Kent decided to visit her daughter, who lived in the next street, one May morning. The estate in Leigh, Lancashire, was overlooked by a hill. It was 6.15 am and she needed a new pair of tights for work. As Mrs Kent walked around the edge of the estate, she was suddenly aware of a figure watching her from just beneath the brow of the hill.

'He' was wearing a one-piece silver suit with a cloak tied at the neck, and raised, pointed lapels. On his head was a cone-shaped hat whilst boot tops were just visible above the line of grass. To the right of the entity stood a large silver spherical object, which cast a bright beam of light down the hill side.

Hurrying on, feeling intimidated by the being, when she arrived at her daughter's Mrs Kent said nothing. On her return a few minutes later, the bright object and the strange figure were still there, so she took a different route back to the house. When she went for her bus half an hour later, the hill was deserted as normal. Mrs Kent died a few years later from cancer.

Small entities with wings were a feature of a case from January 1979 in Rowley Regis, West Midlands. Having seen her husband off to work at 6 am, Mrs Jean Hingley was attracted to the car port by an orange light. It turned out to be a large orange sphere hovering over the garden. As she was watching this, three small figures just over a metre tall shot past her into the house. They wore silver suits and 'goldfish bowl' helmets. More interestingly, they possessed large, gossamer thin oval wings decorated with glittering dots. Thin streamers hung down from their shoulders, and each figure was surrounded by a halo. Their limbs had neither hands nor feet and were silvery-green.

They spoke in unison, telling Mrs Hingley they had come 'from the sky', but would not harm her. When they touched items in the room, the objects levitated. They asked for 'water', so Mrs Hingley brought a tray with glasses, water, plates and mince pies. The entities returned the glasses to her empty, although she did not see them drink. Finally they left, each carrying a mince pie, and boarded the craft, which was still hovering outside. When it had gone, Mrs Hingley felt very ill, and suffered the effects for some time. These included severe headaches.

To counter the argument that this was just an hallucination, investigator Alfred Budden found that the encounter generated some very real environmental effects. These ranged from clear marks left on the ground beneath where the UFO had hovered and damage to various electrical equipment in the house to audio cassettes which were left distorted after the entities handled them.

There are more subtle clues that link the fairies of the past with the aliens of current times, as veteran researcher Jacques Vallee discovered. He used the 1961 Wisconsin, Eagle River case to make an historical comparison.

A sixty-year-old chicken farmer called Joe Simonton found a saucer-shaped object hovering outside his home. Three 'men', who resembled Italians, were inside it. Around one-and-a-half metres tall with dark hair and skin, they wore blue knitted suits, which included a turtle neck top and helmet.

At their request, the chicken farmer gave them a jug of water. One of the entities was cooking on 'a flameless grill of some sort'. After expressing an interest in the food, Joe was handed three small flat cakes.

When the craft departed, Joe Simonton reported the incident to the authorities. The local sheriff attested to Joe's honesty. Astronomer Dr J. Allen Hynek and two other Air Force investigators reported, 'There is no question that Mr Simonton felt that his contact had been a real experience.' At the request of the USAF, the cakes were sent away for analysis in the Food and Drug Laboratory of the US Department of Health, Education and Welfare.

It was discovered that they contained terrestrial ingredients, but surprisingly lacked salt. Vallee pointed out that during encounters with fairy folk, small cakes were often exchanged for water, and that the Gentry could not abide salt. Apparently, neither could Joe Simonton's alien visitors!

These examples show that the Little People of old became the extraterrestrials of more recent years. *Why, then, in the 1980s did the menagerie of 'extraterrestrials' give way to a bug-eyed, hairless dwarf which became known as the 'Gray', named after the insipid colour of its skin?*

Like most cultural trends, the Grays came across from the United States. Until that time, Britain, mainland Europe and other places around the world had reported a wide variety of beings, including 'Nordics' – tall, slim, human-looking aliens with straight, blond hair. The Grays were popularised by American abduction researcher Budd Hopkins in his books, but they then began cropping up everywhere and reports of the other alien types began to dwindle. However, Hopkins and his contemporaries did not 'invent' the Gray. The main feature of this being – its black, impenetrable, large, almond-shaped eyes – had been encountered many times before, even in descriptions of some of the more human-like entities.

The Gray became the dominant image, a coalescence in the human psyche of what an extraterrestrial should look like. The intelligences behind the UFO phenomenon took that image and made it reality. Before that, they had simply transposed the elves and goblins of fairy lore into a futuristic space-age scenario. The Grays represented a refinement, an idea that evolved from our own expectations and fears, a being that exhibited cold, unemotional behaviour, reflecting the attitude of human scientists dealing with lab rats.

The ability of the entities to shape-shift has been known about for centuries. Evans Wentz was told this during his investigations almost a hundred years ago by what today we would term a 'contactee':

> They are able to appear in different forms. One once appeared to me and seemed only four feet high [123 centimetres] and stoutly built. He said: 'I am bigger than I appear now. We can make the old young, the big small, the small big.'

Religious theologians believe that Satan does not have a body. In order to manifest in our world, he forms a body from other materials to interact physically with humans. American abductee Whitley Strieber shared with me his thoughts on this matter, saying, 'When the visitors come to our world they wear bodies as we would wear a diving suit to explore the alien environment of the ocean bed.'

The aliens are here. They are not from outer space, but somewhere much nearer home. After 1850 and the onset of the industrial revolution, the number of contacts between elves and fairies diminished as the beings adapted to a new technological role, and took to the air.

2

The Development of Alien Activity

The Mysterious Airships

The authorities had been aware of alien activity as far back as the late nineteenth century. Interestingly, when they believed UFOs were the invention of eccentric scientists or foreign powers, officials did not question the *reality* of the phenomenon. From 1880 until just before World War One mysterious airships were sighted across the USA, Europe and as far away as New Zealand.

Could terrestrial technology explain these sightings? While it is true the first powered, manned dirigible was flown in September 1852 progress went falteringly after that. It was not until 1903 that fully controlled flight took place, and eleven years later before the US Army built and tested its first airship, the *California Arrow*.

At this time, the Germans launched their first military attack using a Zeppelin against the Dutch. But these man-made airships were a pale reflection of the magnificent flying machines reported over that thirty-year period. Indeed, the majority of sightings occurred while dirigibles were still struggling to get off the drawing board. It was as if the forces behind the phenomenon had taken the basic *idea* of the airship and used it to mock our own feeble efforts by producing something marvellous and magical.

Airships were a new and exciting prospect for the Victorian age, hot on the heels of the industrial revolution. When they began to appear in large numbers it made sense to attribute them to other countries or the work of secret inventors. This was 'logical' and 'rational'. Furthermore, it was a belief encouraged by the airship pilots, just as today UFO entities lead abductees and close encounter participants to assume they are dealing with extraterrestrials. It is all part of the game.

The phenomenon first emerged when the *Santa Fe Daily New Mexican* reported that on March 26, 1880, a cigar-shaped craft driven by a huge propeller was seen by three men. The witnesses described how the occupants of the craft seemed drunken, shouting down at them in an unknown language and throwing items overboard. These included a beautiful flower, a slip of silk-like paper with oriental-looking letters on it, and a cup of 'very peculiar workmanship'. The items were displayed at a nearby railway depot. Within hours, a stranger arrived who asked to examine them, claiming they were of Asiatic origin. The caller said he was a 'collector of curiosities', and made the depot manager an offer of money he could not refuse. Like modern day Men In Black, the stranger managed to procure the evidence and then disappeared.

Two months later, Mr Lee Fore Brace, a passenger on the British India Company's steamer *Patna*, Captain Avern and Third Officer Manning witnessed two strange 'enormous luminous wheels' which appeared on either side of the ship. Brace estimated that they were 'some five hundred to six hundred yards [457–549 metres] in diameter', and revolved slowly.

There were many more sightings, but most were concentrated around the turn of the century. In 1897 came several airship reports from Norway and Sweden. One of these featured a mysterious 'balloon' with an 'electric' or phosphorescent sheen.

Between November 1896 and May 1897, sightings were made in over nineteen states across America. Witnesses described large, elongated aluminium-like objects with bright searchlights, sometimes with wings and propellers, which flew against the wind, silent except for a hissing or humming sound. These cigar-shaped objects are reminiscent of more modern UFO sightings, except they were adorned with paraphernalia fitting the technological expectations of the times.

Captain James Hooten, a railway conductor, had a Close Encounter of the Third Kind with a grounded airship while hunting in Homan, Arkansas. Killing time while waiting for the arrival of a 'special' in Texarkana, Hooten was returning to the railway station when he heard 'a sound for all the world like the working of an air pump on a locomotive'. He made his way through the bush into a clearing where an astonishing sight met his eyes. 'I decided this was the famous airship seen by so many people,' Hooten later told the *Arkansas Gazette*.

He approached a man tinkering at the back of the ship, who wished him good day. At that point, three or four other men emerged from the keel. They allowed Hooten to inspect the craft: 'A close examination showed that the keel was divided into two parts, terminating in front like the sharp edge of a knife-like edge, while the side of the ship bulged gradually towards the middle, and then receded. There were three large wheels upon each side made of some bending metal, and arranged so that they became concave as they moved forwards.'

When the railway conductor enquired as to the motive power of the airship, he was told 'we are using condensed air and aeroplanes, but you will know more later on'. Repairs complete, the crew disappeared below decks and Hooten observed the object making ready to fly:

> Just in front of each wheel, a two-inch tube began to spurt air on the wheels and they commenced revolving. The ship gradually arose with a hissing sound. The aeroplanes suddenly sprang forward, turning their sharp end sky-wards, then the rudders at the end of the ship began to veer to one side and the wheels revolved so fast that one could scarcely see the blades. In less time than it takes to tell, the ship had gone out of sight.

This incident parallels more recent CE3s, particularly those of the 1960s and 1970s. Witnesses often recounted how they came across a grounded UFO 'by accident', with some sort of mechanical problem. Like Hooten, they would be given a vague explanation of the 'spacecraft's' motive power. In Hooten's case, it was tailored to his own understanding, and the technological level of the times. Those who encounter 'extraterrestrials' are given similar waffle about electromagnetic motors. It seems that these apparent random events are especially staged for the benefit of the witnesses, who then report their experiences to the outside world, reinforcing whatever belief the phenomenon wishes to encourage at any particular time.

There were many other recorded encounters between astonished witnesses and human-like airship crew. The self-confessed secret inventors often declared they would unveil their marvellous flying machines to the world 'in the near future', but were never heard of again. Visiting aliens make the same promise, but they, like the airship pilots, never keep their word. *'The spirits lie'*, according to the 18th century Swedish mystic Emanuel Swedenborg.

What the American government made of these mysterious encounters is hard to say as official documentation is not available for that period. No doubt the military were keen to trace the inventors to save themselves years of experimentation and research. One or two individuals did come forward claiming to have built the airships, but they turned out to be publicity seekers and nothing more.

Researcher Carl Grove uncovered details of a flap lasting for several months across Britain during 1909. It prompted headlines in the *East Anglian Daily Times* on May 21 which read: BRITAIN INVADED! AIRSHIPS IN EAST ANGLIA, WALES, AND MIDLANDS. PHANTOM FLEET. NORWICH AND SOUTHEND PAID A VISIT. The article spoke of a 'fleet' of 'cigar-shaped machines with quivering lights and whirring mechanisms' being sighted in Southend, Norwich, Birmingham, Tasburgh, Wroxham, Pontypool and London on the previous Wednesday evening. A number of railwaymen described seeing an object shaped like a policeman's truncheon over West Green in the capital city. A typical sighting occurred in Norwich, and was reported by several people.

A Mrs Turner was returning from the theatre when 'a flash of light came on me all of a sudden, and made the street look like day. I could hear a noise like the whirring of wheels. I looked up, and there I could see a big star of light in front and a big searchlight behind. It was flying very low, so low that it would have touched the pinnacle of Angel Road School had it passed directly over it.' There were two other witnesses in the street.

Half an hour later, around midnight, Mr Chatten, a grocery assistant, was cycling home when he was 'dazzled by a bright light shining from right above me. The trees and hedges were lit brilliantly. I have seen a naval searchlight at Harwich, and I should suppose that what I saw was something of that sort, but there was a bluish tinge about it. It seemed to be switched off after only a few seconds. Getting off my bicycle, I saw a long cigar-shaped object. It was soaring upwards, the tapering end going foremost, and was moving rapidly. On the underside was what I should call a bar, supporting a sort of framework, a yellow light shining at each end.'

That same month several Cardiff docks workmen sighted an airship over the town. Just hours before, a Punch and Judy man had a close encounter while travelling over Caerphilly Mountain. Mr C. Lethbridge told the *South Wales Daily News* that he came across a cigar-shaped object at the side of the road. Two military-looking men were apparently tinkering with it. When they noticed Lethbridge, they jumped into the object jabbering in an unknown foreign language. It then took off rapidly, heading towards Cardiff, making a whirring noise. Residents in nearby Cathays said they saw something resembling an airship at the time indicated by the Punch and Judy man.

The Swedish newspaper *Dagens-Nyheter* reported how on August 24 'an unknown controllable airship' twice circled the Estonian city of Tallin before flying off towards Finland. Exactly a month later, a winged machine passed over Castle Forest near Gothenburg in Sweden.

In Britain the craft were believed to be German reconnaissance ships. Arnold Lupton, MP for Sleaford in Lincolnshire and an explosives expert, sought to put people's minds at rest in the pages of the *South Wales Daily News*, regarding a possible air attack. He pointed out it would require ten thousand pounds of dynamite to destroy the Bank of England. As this would necessitate a large fleet of airships, it obviously was not practical, Lupton told the British public.

The mystery airships made one final appearance in 1913, and then, in that form at least, were gone forever. At that time Winston Churchill asked a question in Parliament about the aerial visitors. Another twenty years passed before official investigations into UFOs began, not in Britain or the USA, but in Scandinavia.

Ghost Fliers Of The Skies

It was prompted by a multitude of sightings involving large grey aircraft during the early 1930s. These mystery machines bore no markings and ran rings around the military authorities in Finland, Norway and Sweden. They out-performed flying craft of that period and operated in impossible weather conditions.

The parish priest of Lantrask in Sweden reported that one had overflown the area around a dozen times between 1932 and 1933.

It flew so low he was able to ascertain that it carried no markings. On one occasion when it passed over the parsonage he saw two figures in the cabin.

During Christmas of 1933 the phenomenon intensified, with many reports across Norway and Sweden describing grey single winged aircraft, which shone down searchlights and executed death-defying manoeuvres. On December 28, the 4th Swedish Flying Corps began liaising with local police forces in a futile attempt to apprehend the rogue pilots who were flagrantly invading that country's airspace. That they were convinced of the reality of the 'ghost fliers' was demonstrated by a statement made by Major-General Reuterswaerd, Commanding General of Upper Norrland, released on April 30, 1934:

> Comparisons of these reports show that there can be no doubt about illegal air traffic over our secret military areas. There are many reports from reliable people which describe close observation of the enigmatic flier. And in every case the same remark can be noted: no insignias or identifying marks were visible on the machines ... The question is: who or whom are they, and why have they been invading our air territory?

Earlier, the head of the Air Force, Major Von Porat, admitted, 'Specific details on this affair cannot be published.'

The Swedish and Norwegian governments were convinced they were dealing with a foreign power, the Russians and Germans being firm favourites. They believed the invaders were interested in locating the positions of their forts and other military installations for a future war. However, an examination of the facts casts grave doubt on this 'obvious' and 'logical' explanation.

Although the technology for searchlights had been available since the end of the nineteenth century, it required heavy batteries aircraft of that period would have found impossible to carry. Aircraft had not progressed much since World War One. Most were clumsy bi-planes with open cockpits and no radios. The range of these dinosaurs was very limited. It would have required a string of manned fuel bases to keep them in the air over Scandinavia.

Despite intensive searches by ground soldiers and ships belonging to Sweden and Norway, no bases were found.

At the time of the sightings, Adolf Hitler was secretly building up the Luftwaffe, but would he have risked his meagre number of ex-World War One pilots in pointless missions over Scandinavia? The large grey aircraft were sometimes seen in threes. Amazingly, the ghost fliers seemed immune to accident, even in atrocious weather conditions. This could not be said for their Swedish persuers. On one occasion when the 4th Flying Corps tried to shadow the mystery aircraft over mountains they lost two bi-planes. Finally, the Scandinavian authorities turned their backs on the phenomenon, and as if deciding the game had run its course, the mystery fliers left.

Several years later during World War Two, the 'alien' craft were back, harassing Allied and Axis pilots alike. This time, they mani-fested as the soon to be familiar futuristic-looking discs and as balls of intelligently controlled light.

The Foo Fighters

Researcher Hilary Evans uncovered a sighting which occurred on October 14, 1943, involving air crew of the American 384th. Bombing an industrial plant at Schweinfurt, Germany, on their final run many crew members saw 'a cluster of discs' straight ahead. They were described as 'silver coloured, about one inch thick and three inches in diameter, gliding down slowly' in a tight group. One B-17 pilot feared collision as he was unable to take evasive action, but the bomber flew through the tiny objects and carried on unhindered.

It is tempting to explain this report as nothing more than 'chaff', pieces of aluminium foil released by aircraft to confuse enemy radar. But if this was so, why did the bomber crews fail to recognise it? After all, it would have been released by their own aircraft. Such a 'misidentification' would not have warranted the official investiga-tions that followed by concerned intelligence agencies. The sighting of miniature UFOs is not unique. There are many incidents featuring small craft, but these are less often reported, and hardly feature in mainstream UFO literature.

On August 20, 1965, the Inca stone fortress of Sacsahuaman, near Cuzco, Peru was the location for an encounter with a small disc. It was around noon when engineer Alberto Ugarte, his wife, their friend Elwin Voter and a party of other people witnessed a silver disc around four-and-a-half feet in diameter land on a nearby terrace. Two small beings emerged, strangely shaped and of a dazzling brightness. They must have decided there were too many spectators about and retreated inside, whereupon the object took off and disappeared westwards.

Most of the sightings reported by air crew during World War Two featured balls of light rather than nuts and bolts craft. The phenomenon became so common they were given the name 'foo fighters', from the French word *feu*, meaning 'fire'. The Allies thought the objects were secret weapons belonging to the Germans, but after the war they discovered the Luftwaffe pilots were just as mystified, and had called them *feuer* balls.

These foo fighters sound suspiciously like astronomical phenomena such as fire ball meteors, or the rare phenomenon of ball lightning, except for one irrefutable fact: pilots reported that the objects seemed to be under intelligent control, playing tag with aircraft and making right angled turns.

An American B-29 bomber belonging to the 486 Bomb Group, 792 Squadron was flying near Sumata in Indonesia on August 10, 1944, when its crew had such an encounter. Captain Alvah Reida later filed a detailed report where he described how a red-orange sphere appeared off the starboard wing, flying parallel with the aircraft. The crew attempted to shake it off by taking evasive manoeuvres, but the object kept pace with their every turn. After several minutes, it suddenly shot away at a ninety-degree angle and accelerated off into the night. Reida told intelligence agents he thought it was 'some new type of radio controlled missile or weapon'.

One of the most celebrated cases involved the American 415 fighter squadron who flew from Dijon in France on the night of November 23, 1944, on an intercept mission to Strasbourg and Mannheim. Lieutenant Edward Schlueter, Lieutenant Don Myers and Intelligence Officer Lieutenant Ringwald were flying over the Vosges Mountains when Ringwald pointed out around ten orange-red balls moving in formation at great velocity. The crew speculated whether they were stars or meteors, and discarding these possible explanations, decided to give chase. As they closed in, the objects just melted into nothing, only to reappear minutes later before vanishing again. The crew tired of the game of tag, eventually gave up and carried on with their mission.

A former prisoner of war held at the Heydebreck camp in Upper Silesia, Poland, reported a sighting which occurred on January 22, 1945. He was one of a number of men paraded by the Germans before being marched away to evade the liberating Russian army. A bomber appeared overhead with what appeared at first to be fire at its stern. As the men watched in horror, they realised it was, in fact, a silver ball on the tail of the aircraft, which was desperately trying to evade the alien intruder. Both objects disappeared from sight.

There were many other sightings of foo fighters. Incongruously, pilots discovered that the objects did not appear on either their own on-board radar equipment or ground-based stations. Foo fighters continued to harass both Allied and Axis pilots until the end of the war.

On The Trail Of The Ghost Rockets

Foo fighters were largely forgotten with the ending of the war, but just months later a new wave of UFO sightings hit the headlines. The place was Scandinavia, location of the mysterious grey aircraft ten years previously. This time, witnesses reported anomalous lights and rocket-shaped objects. Once again, the media and the authorities assumed they originated from enemy territory.

When lights were first sighted on February 26, 1946, in the north of Finland, they were explained as 'inordinate meteor activity' by Helsinki radio. By late May, they had spread southwards into Sweden, where almost daily reports were made. The sightings escalated throughout the summer. By autumn, nine hundred and ninety-six were officially recorded by the Swedish defence authorities. Unofficially, the reports were put at several thousand.

These nocturnal lights were seen emitting flames from their rear, travelling at speeds ranging from 'rapid' to 'sedate'. The lights may have just been the visible portion of hard nuts and bolts objects, judging by descriptions given of craft made during daylight. Witnesses described missile or dark lozenge-shaped objects, often spouting a short tail of flame, which flew horizontally before sometimes falling vertically, although no explosions were ever heard. Mixed in with these reports were descriptions of egg and spinning top shapes, more reminiscent of modern-day UFOs.

A meteorologist was in the right place at the right time to make an observation, through his telescope, of an object passing over Stockholm. During his ten second observation the scientist noticed it was 'at least ninety feet long. The body was torpedo-shaped and shining like metal. It had a tapered tail that spewed glowing blue and green smoke and a series of fireballs.'

A hitherto secret telegram sent from the US Embassy in Stockholm on July 11, 1946, illustrates how seriously the phenomenon was being treated, and speculates on the origin of the ghost rockets:

For some weeks there have been reports of strange rocket-like missiles being seen in Swedish and Finnish skies. During the past few days, reports of such objects being seen have greatly increased. Members of Legation saw one Tuesday afternoon. One landed on a beach near Stockholm same afternoon without causing any damage and according to press, fragments are now being studied by military authorities. Local scientists on first inspection stated it contained organic substance resembling carbide.

Defence staff last night issued communiqué listing various places where missiles had been observed and urging public report all mysterious sound and light phenomena. Press this afternoon announces one such missile fell in Stockholm suburb. Missile observed by member Legation made no sound and seemed to be falling rapidly to earth. No sound of explosion followed, however.

Military Attaché is investigating through Swedish channels and has been promised results Swedish observations. Swedes profess ignorance as to origin, character or purpose of missiles, but state definitely they are not launched by Swedes. Eyewitness reports state missiles came in from southerly direction, proceeding to northwest. Six units Atlantic Fleet under Admiral Hewitt arrived Stockholm this morning. If missiles are of Soviet origin as generally believed, purpose might be political to intimidate Swedes ...

Examination of substances at alleged crash sites turned out to be ambiguous, and probably unconnected with the phenomenon. Nevertheless, this did not detract from how seriously the sightings were treated. A month after the telegram, the *New York Times* reported that 'the Swedish General Staff described the situation as "extremely dangerous"'. Military experts from Britain and the United States were despatched to Sweden.

The authorities were convinced the Russians were testing sophisticated V-2 rockets developed by captured German scientists. United States' aerial warfare intelligence expert General David Sarnoff decided after studying all the data that the flying objects were neither mythological nor meteorological, but 'real missiles'. In their zeal to offer a 'rational' explanation, the authorities missed something obvious. *Despite the thousands of reports, not one 'missile' had crashed and caused either structural damage or fatalities.*

When Professor R. V. Jones, Britain's Air Staff Director of Intelligence and scientific adviser to MI6, examined the reports he poured scorn on the belief that the objects were Russian missiles. He said the supposedly flying bombs flew at twice the range the Germans had achieved, and even with credit for the highest reliability at least ten missiles should have crashed in Sweden. The professor believed that *all* the sightings had a meteorological explanation.

It seems that Professor Jones' views were not shared by anyone else in the intelligence community because in late August the Scandinavian media were ordered to tone down or cease altogether their reporting of the ghost rockets, and instead to forward all sightings to the relevant intelligence department. An official enquiry into the affair was ordered.

The Swedish government released the results in October 1946. They estimated that out of the one thousand cases they studied, eighty per cent were attributable to 'celestial phenomena'. However, there were around two hundred cases where objects had been tracked on radar 'which cannot be the phenomena of nature or products of the imagination, nor can be referred to as Swedish airplanes'. Neither did the authors of the report believe these objects were V-type bombs. In other words, a sizeable percentage remained *unidentified*.

A month before the results of the study were published, the phenomenon surfaced outside Scandinavia, with sightings in Macedonia and Salonika. The following year, the ghost rockets caused consternation in Greece, Portugal, Tangier and Italy. A scientific study in Greece headed by Professor Paul Santorini similarly could not find a 'rational' solution to the phenomenon.

The development of alien activity was about to take a further twist, matched by an increase in government secrecy as officials struggled – and failed – to grasp the complexities of the phenomenon.

3

The Secret Inquiry in America

The Aliens Emerge

It was in 1947 that the UFO phenomenon gained common currency as being of extraterrestrial origin. Until then, explanations included atmospheric and astronomical phenomena, and new advanced aircraft built in secret by lone eccentric inventors, the Armed Forces or a foreign terrestrial power. It is amazing how inventive sceptical scientists and military authorities can be in their attempts to explain away every sighting. History teaches us that lesson most vividly.

Probably the first full scale official investigation of a UFO sighting occurred in Japan in 1235. On September 24, General Yoritsume was camped with his army when several lights were observed acrobating around in the south-western sky. The phenomenon lasted all night, after which the General ordered an investigation. Officials took statements, consulted 'experts' and eventually made their report. 'The whole thing is completely natural, General,' they said. 'It is only the wind making the stars sway.'

Then, as now, despite the best attempts of 'experts' there has always been a hard-core of cases which cannot be swept away as misidentifications of the planet Venus, ball lightening, meteors or the wind simply making the stars sway! This hard core, about ten per cent of all reports, included sightings of nuts and bolts craft by reliable witnesses, who described how the intruders made 'impossible' manoeuvres and moved at death-defying speeds. In more recent times, objects were often tracked on radar and in some instances observed in the air by military and commercial pilots.

The belief in some quarters that residual UFO reports were sightings of advanced top secret aircraft was supplemented with a new theory in the late 1940s. At that time, the relatively new genre of science fiction was just beginning to reach a wider audience with its lurid tales of invading bug-eyed monsters from outer space. The general public began to speculate that something of that sort might actually be happening! Supporters pointed out that the sudden right angled turns made by the craft would crush human pilots because of the terrific gravity forces created by such manoeuvres. If the objects were manned, it was with an intelligent species built of much sterner stuff.

The second reason for this change in perception was that the objects now looked 'space age'. The cigar shape remained, but was now unadorned and more sleek looking. Gone were the propellers and other paraphernalia of the airship period. It was no longer perceived as a Russian rocket, but referred to by those in the know as a 'mother ship'. But sightings of the cigar were overtaken by reports of shiny metallic discs.

These were popularised in June 1947 when civilian pilot Kenneth Arnold saw nine crescent-shaped objects flying over the Cascade Mountains in Washington State. He told reporters they moved 'like saucers skipping across water'. The unfortunate term 'flying saucer' now came into common use and has dogged serious research into the phenomenon ever since.

The new belief that UFOs were space vehicles was further bolstered just over a week after Arnold's historic sighting when news broke of a 'saucer' which had crashed on a ranch near Roswell in New Mexico, scattering tiny alien bodies. The subsequent cover-up and feeble explanation of a balloon caused a controversy that rumbles on to this day. There is no doubt that the Arnold 'saucers' and the Roswell crash were crucial in the shift of public perception to visitors from outer space. In retrospect, I feel that both events were staged by the intelligences behind the phenomenon to reinforce this particular belief.

Roswell has been extensively written about in the last decade, with films and documentaries in its wake. I was even involved in giving a pre-performance lecture for an opera based on the case, which toured parts of England. In truth, the story seems to grow with the telling, and has not been helped with the emergence of highly suspicious cine film supposedly showing an alien autopsy. However, it is worth giving some basic facts about the incident.

The Roswell Crash

On the night of 2 July, during a thunder storm, William Brazel heard an explosion above his ranch in New Mexico. It sounded so unlike thunder that the following day he and a neighbour rode out to check. They were astounded to discover a deep gouge in the earth as if an object had skidded there, and some wreckage strewn over an area more than a kilometre wide. The debris included a lightweight metal which was extremely tough, beams that resembled balsa wood but which would not burn, and sheets of parchment-like material. Some of the debris bore hieroglyphic or geometric symbols.

Thinking it could be the remains of a secret prototype aircraft, Brazel took a sample of the material to Roswell and spoke to the sheriff. Two deputies went out to investigate the rancher's story and found a burnt circle on the ground. Brazel was directed to the town's air base, and Major Jesse Marcel and a junior intelligence officer were put onto the case. They loaded up some of the remains onto the back of a truck and took them back to the base. The area was cordoned off by the military while they collected every bit of debris. Brazel was taken to Roswell and put under 'voluntary' house arrest for a week.

In the meantime, the media were alerted when base officer Lieutenant Walter Haut issued a press release informing the world that Roswell Army Air Field 'was fortunate enough to gain possession of a disc.' Local newspapers and radio picked up on the story, but were then ordered to drop it by the Pentagon when they decided to put the lid on it.

Unable to identify the wreckage at Roswell, Colonel William Blanchard ordered Major Marcel to load it into a B29 and fly it to Wright Patterson Air Force Base. At this point, General Roger Ramay took control and claimed that the whole episode had been a silly mistake. He held a press conference and produced the remains of a weather balloon, claiming that was the debris which had been recovered from the Brazel ranch. When the rancher was brought in front of the media he backed up the story, having been rehearsed beforehand by Ramay.

In 1978 Marcel, now retired, told investigating ufologists that the balloon was a cover story to hide the fact that the military had no idea *what* the debris was. He affirmed that the wreckage had unusual properties. For instance, there were a large number of

43

pieces of 'tin foil' which, although paper thin, could not be permanently bent, even with a sledge hammer. Neither would it burn. Other witnesses have backed up his claims.

Around 1950, another angle to the story emerged. It involved a civil engineer with the Soil Conservation Service, called Grady Barnett. He told friends he had been working near Socorro, about a hundred miles west of the Brazel ranch, at the time of the incident. Barnett claimed he saw a crashed disc in the desert with a number of small, hairless humanoids scattered about close by – obviously dead. A group of archaeology students led by a professor were also there. Before they could do anything, the military arrived and the witnesses were ordered in no uncertain terms to keep quiet about what they had seen.

The bodies were taken to Wright Patterson in a B29, where rumour has it they were later transferred to Area 51 in the Tonopah Air Base, situated in a remote region of Nevada. According to some commentators, the American military back-engineered the Roswell saucer and other retrieved UFOs and test flew them over Area 51. Some intriguing videos have been taken in recent years of flying objects over the base.

Some researchers, like nuclear physicist Stanton Freidman, believe that a UFO was struck by lightening over the Brazel Ranch, whereupon it lost altitude and hit the desert, scattering wreckage before bouncing up again and finally crashing near Socorro.

Around a hundred and fifty witnesses were traced, but Grady Barnett passed away before he could be interviewed whilst none of the supposed archaeology students and their tutor came forward. This makes the second part of the story highly speculative. However, Glenn Dennis, a Roswell mortician, has claimed that the air base contacted him at the time enquiring about preserving body tissue and the availability of small coffins. A base nurse told Dennis she had been involved in preparing the transportation of child-sized bodies. In 1982, 'Pappy' Henderson, the pilot of the B-29, said he took the corpses to Wright Patterson.

There is no doubt that *something highly unusual* did crash in the New Mexican desert on July 3, 1947. Veteran ufologist John Keel suggested that a Japanese balloon bomb was to blame. These were sent across to bomb the United States during World War Two. How such a device could stay in the atmosphere for twenty-four months, and why it should remain a secret over fifty years, is not explained.

Another suggestion was that a secret high altitude balloon called a Mogul had been hit by lightening and crashed. But again, why all the secrecy? Despite this, the debris was obviously ambiguous enough to allow theories like this to be considered. Evans Wentz was told that the Little People wanted us to believe in them, but not too much – just enough, it seems, for them to influence society without dominating it.

In 1995 when the General Accounting Office of the US government revealed the results of their independent enquiry into Roswell, it was disclosed that they were unable to find hundreds of files relevant to the enquiry. These had 'disappeared'.

This sudden explosion of alien activity should have alerted covert government departments and initiated a scientific study and investigation of the UFO phenomenon. This is exactly what happened, but were the authorities just playing safe by covering every avenue of enquiry, or does it mean they had firm reason to believe that alien activity was a reality – evidence which perhaps included wreckage and even bodies?

As the phenomenon evolved over the next few decades, it presented a challenge that could not be ignored even by the most sceptical. It was seemingly capable of coming and going with impunity, violating the free will of individuals and subtly controlling and moulding the belief systems of society. As governments like to give the impression *they* are in control, it makes sense they would take seriously anything that posed a threat to themselves or their minions. Despite denials, government departments around the world *have* taken an active interest in UFO-related incidents. This is all a matter of record, but the exact nature and depth of that concern remains controversial.

The Secret Enquiry Begins
Throughout much of the latter half of the twentieth century, representatives of the security services publicly denied any interest in the UFO phenomenon. Until recently, our own Ministry of Defence regularly issued the bizarre statement that they were not in the business of investigating UFO reports 'because they pose no defence implica-

tions'. In 1972, FBI Director J. Edgar Hoover claimed that 'The investigation of Unidentified Flying Objects is not – and never has been – a matter that is within the investigative jurisdiction of the FBI.' Yet when the American Freedom of Information Act came into force in 1976, previously 'Top Secret' documents proved this was untrue.

While they were in denial, it transpired that the Criminal Intelligence Agency, Defense Intelligence Agency, National Security Agency and the Federal Bureau of Investigation *were* keeping a sharp eye on our 'alien' intruders. In the early nineteen sixties when Senator Barry Goldwater tried to access UFO files stored by the USAF, he was told they were still classified 'Above Top Secret'. Wilbert Smith, a senior radio engineer working for the Canadian Government, wrote a hitherto top secret memorandum in November 1950 which stated that UFOs were 'the most highly classified subject in the United States, rating higher even than the H-bomb'.

It is blatantly obvious from the contents of declassified documents that the US Air Force took the UFO phenomenon very seriously indeed, particularly when reports were made by professional observers. A document dating from December 1948 entitled 'Analysis of Flying Object Incidents in the US' contains the following comments:

> A number of reports on unidentified flying objects come from observers who, because of their technical background and experience, do not appear to be influenced by unfounded sensationalism nor inclined to report explainable phenomena as new types of airborne devices.

In April 1947, two employees of the Weather Bureau Station at Richmond, Virginia, had three sightings of 'a strange metallic disc'. While monitoring a weather balloon, through a theodolite they observed an object for fifteen seconds. It was, said the Top Secret report, 'shaped like an ellipse with a flat bottom and a round top. It appeared below the balloon and was much larger in size. The disc appeared to be moving rather rapidly.'

Another file from June of that year told how an Air Force lieutenant flying north-west of Lake Meade, Nevada, observed 'five or six white circular objects in close formation and travelling at an estimated speed of two hundred and eighty five miles per hour'. The following day, two scientists and another witness saw 'a large disc or sphere moving horizontally at high speed and an estimated altitude of ten thousand feet. It was of uniform shape and had no protruding surfaces such as wings.' They were on Highway 17 heading towards the White Sands V-2 firing grounds in New Mexico.

Clearly, the authorities were impressed by some UFO sightings. What did they do about them? What were their conclusions, publicly or privately? Much has emerged in recent years which goes some way to answering these questions. At the time of writing, Britain still does not have a Freedom of Information Act so we must rely mainly on the Americans to give us a clue to what is undoubtedly a world-wide picture.

In the wake of the Kenneth Arnold sighting, eight hundred and fifty new reports of strange aerial objects were made in just two months. Obviously, many of these were misidentifications, but Arnold's bravery – or foolhardiness – in going public encouraged many other people to do the same who otherwise would have remained silent to avoid ridicule. The result of all this activity culminated in a secret investigation by the US Air Force.

In July 1947, Brigadier General George Schulgen, an Army/Air Force Intelligence Officer, requested military bases and intelligence agencies to co-operate in collating UFO reports. As a result of this, E. G. Fitch of the FBI circulated a memo to agents headed 'Flying Discs' in which he informed them of Schulgen's determination to 'ascertain whether the flying discs are a fact', and if so to 'learn all about them'. According to Fitch, Schulgen was working from the premise that the objects were a 'foreign body, mechanically devised and controlled'.

The FBI debated whether or not it was prepared to spend time and money on the project. Finally, despite reservations, J. Edgar Hoover gave the go-ahead, instructing his agents to co-operate with the military. The arrangement was to last barely a month whereupon the FBI discovered they were being given all the poor quality cases, leaving the Air Force to conduct the serious work. However, the FBI continued to take an interest in UFOs, despite Hoover's later denial.

An FBI agent based in London reported an incident involving an RAF Mosquito on night flying practise near the Dutch coast when it was ordered to intercept an object tracked on radar. The chase lasted half an hour and concluded over Norfolk when the object took 'efficient, controlled, evasive action'. This was five months before Kenneth Arnold's encounter.

Lieutenant Colonel Donald Springer from Hamilton Field Air Base in California carried out an appraisal of sixteen American cases which occurred between May 19 and July 20, 1947. Ten occurred in daylight, most of them involving high calibre observers. Springer noted: 'This "flying saucer" situation is not all imaginary or seeing too much in some natural phenomenon. Something is really flying around.'

After studying all the Air Force's data, Lieutenant General Nathan Twining, head of Air Material Command, concluded, 'The phenomenon reported is something real and not visionary or fictitious.' Twining suggested the creation of a secret project to gather information which could then be routinely passed on to branches of the military and scientific agencies connected to the government. Schulgen endorsed the idea, and Major General Craigie, chief of staff at the Air Force, gave approval.

Pointing The Way
Project Sign was launched on January 22, 1948, and established at Wright Patterson Air Force Base, Dayton, Ohio. Although the codename was secret, the existence of the project was not. It required reports from the general public as well as professional observers. Therefore, a degree of publicity was inevitable. The media dubbed it 'Project Saucer'. Within days of its launch, Sign became embroiled in a major case.

On January 7, Captain Thomas Mantell died flying his P-51 Mustang aircraft while in pursuit of a 'metallic object … tremendous in size'. As he closed in, radio contact was lost, wreckage later being found along with the dead pilot. Apparently, he blacked out after climbing too high without oxygen equipment. But what was the mysterious object?

Sign was determined to find out, enlisting the help of astronomer Dr J. Allen Hynek. Despite the fact he told them there was not an astronomical explanation, the hierarchy advised the media that Mantell had died 'chasing' the planet Venus – even though it was not visible during the day. Many years later, Hynek turned from being a sceptic to a believer and founded the Centre for UFO Studies.

I met Professor Hynek when he visited England in the early 1980s. While we were driving in my car, he told me the Mantell incident was only the first of many occasions when pressure was put upon him to explain away a UFO sighting as a star, meteor or bright planet, even though it was patently obvious that was not the answer. Hynek was a pleasant, mild mannered scientist, who was only interested in discovering the Truth.

Ironically, it seems possible that Mantell was chasing a Skyhook balloon. At that time, the Navy was secretly testing the devices high in the atmosphere and had not informed the Army/Air Force. Nevertheless, this case illustrates how Sign was determined to explain away everything, no matter how absurd the explanation. Despite this, they quickly realised that some sightings appeared to represent an exotic phenomenon. Even hard line sceptics agreed it was ridiculous to suggest that the USSR would test fly advanced aerial devices over American territory, where they could crash or be captured. At long last the authorities were seeing sense on that one!

Several highly strange cases caused a split in Sign. One faction were certain that *all* sightings could be explained away, but the other faction were equally as adamant that some reports represented alien activity of some sort …

A case that seemed to back the pro-alien faction concerned an Eastern Airlines DC-3 flying on a clear moonlit night over Alabama in the early hours of July 24, 1948. Suddenly, pilot and co-pilot Clarence Chiles and John Whitted were startled by a cigar-shaped object rushing towards them. They took evasive action to avoid a collision, and as the UFO sped by saw it had two rows of 'windows' along the side, which glowed bright blue, and flames shooting from the rear. Chiles estimated the one hundred foot object was just seven hundred feet away when it suddenly put on a burst of speed and zoomed into the clouds. The pilot told investigators they felt 'its prop wash rocking our DC-3'.

About an hour earlier, an engineer at an air base in nearby Georgia had reported an almost identical object, moving horizontally. Dr Hynek was pushed to try and explain the phenomenon as a meteor; but they descend at an angle into the atmosphere and do not move horizontally. The sceptics within Sign were beaten. Captain Edward Ruppelt, who was later to head the Air Force's Project Blue Book, said in 1956 that this case 'shook them worse than the Mantell incident'.

Within two weeks of the Eastern Airlines sighting, the Air Technical Intelligence Center (ATIC) decided to make an 'Estimate of the Situation' report. Ruppelt saw this top secret document before it was destroyed, and confirmed that ATIC concluded that UFOs 'were interplanetary in origin'. It was General Hoyt Vandenberg, the Chief of Staff, who ordered the document be burned after rejecting its conclusions. Vandenberg said it lacked evidence, even though a visit from ATIC operatives to his Pentagon office tried to change his mind.

This put the sceptics back in charge at Sign, and the pro-alien faction was dispersed to other jobs. Sign produced another report stressing how most cases could be explained, while admitting it had failed to find a solution for around twenty per cent of the two hundred and thirty seven cases investigated. The project was downgraded and given a new codename, Grudge, which perhaps summed up the Air Force's attitude towards the UFO problem!

Grudge's remit was simple: to explain away as many UFO sightings as possible. In an attempt to dispense with the mystery, Grudge encouraged responsible journalists to write negative articles, but not everyone was convinced there was nothing to it. Despite its own best efforts, Grudge failed to identify twenty-three per cent of the two hundred and fifty sightings it had assessed up to August 1949. Grudge was put on hold for the next two years or so until Ruppelt took over the reigns.

Little Green Fireballs

In the meantime, a new type of UFO was causing a headache for the authorities. Green fireballs were over-flying top secret missile sites, nuclear research facilities and atomic weapons testing grounds in New Mexico, location of the Roswell UFO crash. The nuclear facility at Los Alamos seemed a particular target. Despite what had been learned by Project Sign, once again the same old questions were trotted out: were the objects a natural phenomenon, Soviet spy aircraft or something else entirely?

Sightings began in November 1948. Brilliant green lights were seen at night and during daylight by military personnel, investigating agents and scientists sent to study the phenomenon. Although superficially they resembled meteors, an official report stated there were 'nine scientific reasons' which proved this was not the case. It concluded that the fireballs were either 'hitherto unobserved natural phenomena or that they were man-made'. The report added that 'no scientific experiments are known to exist in this country which could give rise to such phenomena'. In January 1949, the Navy and Air Force were so worried they organised a joint conference called 'Protection of Vital Installations'. A memo outlining their discussions was sent to FBI director J. Edgar Hoover.

Dr Lincoln La Paz, a world authority on meteorites with top secret clearance, was called in to shed light on the mystery. La Paz and his team of investigators interviewed witnesses and plotted the passage of the green fireballs. However, when they looked for meteorite debris, there was none. Nor was an object seen either before or after appearing over its sighting location. The UFOs were apparently materialising near their 'targets', over flying them at between three and twelve miles a second, then vanishing.

The good doctor had his own sighting when he saw a green fireball moving horizontally across the sky. He measured its light output, analysis suggesting there was a high copper content. This was confirmed when copper dust was found below fireball flight paths. La Paz had no doubts that the fireballs were previously unknown objects. The evidence was examined by leading geophysicist Dr Joseph Kaplan, who later told the Air Force scientific advisory board he found it 'unsettling'.

It was decided to convene a meeting to discuss the findings. The Conference on Aerial Phenomena attracted many scientists, including Edward Teller who helped mastermind the atomic bomb. Amazingly, although invited, Project Grudge did not even think it fit to send a representative!

The conference members were split down the middle. Teller speculated that the phenomena were optical rather than physical, and suggested they might be some sort of electrical plasma. On the other hand, La Paz was certain the objects were neither meteors nor any other sort of natural phenomena. He felt they represented an unknown technology, in which case 'intensive, systematic investigation should not be delayed'.

In the wake of this, Project Twinkle was set up headed by Dr Kaplan to carry out a more detailed scientific study of the Los Alamos UFOs. An automatic camera system was developed to film the fireballs from two different locations. Other devices were obtained which could measure electromagnetic emissions from the objects. The equipment was installed near Holloman Air Force Base in New Mexico for a period of eighteen months between 1950 and 1951.

A number of problems conspired to make the project a failure. Military personnel who had been trained to use the equipment were taken away to fight the Korean War, records were not kept properly, and there was a lack of communication. Perhaps significantly, the green fireballs started playing hide-and-seek games with Twinkle's operatives. The UFOs would disappear from one place and reappear elsewhere. When the equipment was transferred to the new window area, the objects moved on, leading Twinkle by the nose around New Mexico. Were the UFOs really playing a game, or was that just how it appeared? Project Twinkle closed down in late 1951. By 1954, like the airships, the ghost fliers and ghost rockets before them, the green fireballs had gone.

From Grudge To Blue Book

After languishing in the wilderness for two years, Grudge metamorphosed into Project Blue Book. Captain Edward J. Ruppelt took over the reigns in October 1951. It did not take long for him to realise something strange was going on. Just six months into his stewardship a wave of UFOs hit America.

It began in April 1952 and came to a climax in the second half of July. In May, a high ranking member of the CIA was hosting a garden party near its headquarters in Langley, Virginia, when suddenly – to the amazement of his influential guests – a UFO flew directly overhead. It performed an aerial ballet, then disappeared. Ruppelt stamped the file 'Unknown'. The phenomenon seemed out to convince those who mattered of its reality. What followed was a virtual invasion of the airspace above Washington, DC.

A Pan-Am DC-4 flying over Washington on the evening of July 14 had a close encounter with six coin-shaped UFOs. Initially, the objects, which glowed red on top, were below the aircraft, then changed direction and shot upwards past the aircraft. Just a few days later on July 19, radar screens all around the capital started to pick up unidentified blips. It began just before midnight and ceased soon after dawn the following day.

Three radar systems were involved: a long range radar, short range equipment at Washington Airport and a military radar. All three recorded UFOs that night, often simultaneously. The objects would behave like normal aircraft, then suddenly accelerate, one reaching the amazing speed of 7,000 mph! When they started flying through restricted airspace over the White House there was panic. The nearest military installation was undergoing runway repairs, and therefore out of action. At last, one jet interceptor was scrambled, but it was 3 am before it arrived – and by then the UFOs had gone, to re-appear after the aircraft returned to base.

By now civilian aircraft had witnessed the strange lights cavorting around the sky. A Capital Airlines DC-4 was directed towards the objects from radar recordings. The crew had visual confirmation of several UFOs, but when the airliner closed in they shot away and disappeared off the radar screen. Harry Barnes, Senior Radar Controller at Washington Airport, described the behaviour of the UFOs as 'like a bunch of small kids out playing'.

The response of the defence authorities was puzzling, to say the least. Here were unknown aircraft playing games above the country's capital, and when at last they make a response just one solitary jet arrives. No one even informed Blue Book. Ruppelt only learned of the events through reading the morning newspapers!

When he tried to investigate the sightings, all sorts of obstacles were put in his way by the Air Force. It was as if someone high up in the government knew what the UFOs represented and decided to do nothing about it. American researcher Barry Greenwood has suggested that the flap was deliberately left to develop, so as to build up public hysteria. This was the height of the Cold War, but it had been difficult to get citizens voluntarily to participate in ground observer watches. After the Washington episode, recruitment went up and more people were watching the skies.

UFO reports started coming in from all over the country. Just a week later Washington was hit by another wave. Ruppelt was furious when told of this, because the messenger was not the Air Force, but a journalist who wanted to know what he was doing about it. The Blue Book chief despatched three investigators to the airport: they saw many of the objects being tracked on radar. When two F-94 interceptors arrived, an incredible game of cat-and-mouse ensued. The objects disappeared, only to reappear when the aircraft had gone, so more interceptors were scrambled. A single jet was able to get fairly close to one of the UFOs before it shot off at a terrific speed. The pilot, Lieutenant William Patterson, reported: 'I chased a single bright light which I estimated about ten miles away. I lost visual contact with it at about two miles.'

Two days later, the USAF held a press conference, but none of the eye-witnesses attended. Instead, a radar expert was presented. He suggested that the objects were a mirage created by temperature inversions in the atmosphere. Radar experts at Washington Airport disagreed. Neither did the US Weather Bureau back up the 'theory'. Project Blue Book's conclusions were that the reports remained unexplained.

The Robertson Panel

The dramatic displays put on by the UFOs over Washington made it seem they were determined to stamp their reality on our own. Certainly the public furore that followed ensured that the CIA would become more involved. It was Ruppelt who pushed to upgrade the science in Blue Book by suggesting that the Battelle Memorial Institute – a prestigious scientific research facility – become part of the project to carry out intense statistical analysis of the data. This was agreed in early 1952.

The Battelle Institute produced a rigorous, scientific study into 2,199 UFO reports from the Blue Book files. Scientists spent as much time evaluating the witnesses as they did the observations. Special Report 14 was subject to intense secrecy. It concluded that 22 per cent of cases qualified as unknowns. These were accounts where the quality of the data was high.

When the Air Force informed Ruppelt that a panel of scientists would be convened to review the best cases he had no idea the CIA was behind it. The agency had its own agenda, but it was about secrecy, not the scientific evaluation of UFOs. Even Dr Hynek was not allowed to attend many of the meetings because he did not possess security clearance – despite having more experience of investigating UFOs than any other scientist.

The team was headed by Dr H. P. Robertson, a physicist who had been involved in the Manhattan Project, which built the atomic bomb. There were four other scientists on what became known as the Robertson Panel: Dr Luis Alvarez, Dr Lloyd Berkner, Dr Sam Goldsmith and Dr Thornton Page. All of them were connected to the physical sciences, making it clear that the CIA did not believe that UFOs were hallucinations.

Naively, Ruppelt and his colleagues presented thirty cases to the panel which they believed demonstrated that the phenomenon was real, which to Blue Book meant 'extraterrestrial'. Just a few minutes were given to each case. Solutions were offered for some, others were left unexplained. Ruppelt waited for a statement from the Robertson Panel, and was to do so for a long time. The CIA-led statement was top secret, concerned with diffusing public interest in UFOs, not investigating the phenomenon.

They recommended that the government debunk the subject to bring about a 'result in the reduction in public interest in "flying saucers"'. It was even suggested that Walt Disney should make propaganda films, and that the media ought to produce anti-UFO material for broadcast and publication. The aim of their two-year plan was to 'reduce or eliminate' public interest in the phenomenon. But there was a fly in the ointment – the rise in civilian organisations which carried out their own investigations into UFO encounters. Most of these were rank amateurs, but a handful were staffed by members with professional backgrounds, who took their interest very seriously. The CIA recommended that these groups should be infiltrated by their agents.

As files declassified in the 1970s show, the Robertson Panel's ploy was hugely successful. A secret memo dated December 17, 1953, records how 'the definite drop in the number of sightings' was 'attributed to the actions following the recommendations'. Blue Book had been ordered to find explanations – any would do – to reduce the number of 'unknowns'. This resulted in a decline from twenty to one or two per cent. On paper at least, the UFO problem had gone away.

Captain Ruppelt left the Air Force in late 1953, and two years later wrote his memoirs in which he said, 'Maybe I was just the front man for a big cover-up.' However, four years afterwards, Ruppelt recanted, and went from a UFO believer to a sceptic, his faith having been demolished by the rise of the contactee movement, the lunatic fringe of ufology.

Contactees were flamboyant individuals, mostly men, who claimed contact with humanoid 'space brothers', and described rides around the solar system in 'flying saucers'. They grabbed the headlines and stole the show, making it hard for any self- respecting scientist to associate himself with the study of UFOs. Ruppelt was not the only person who had his enthusiasm dented, making it fair to speculate that perhaps the contactee movement had a helping hand from the CIA. Certainly, it played right into their hands.

In 1966, Dr Edward Condon, a quantum physicist who helped build the atom bomb, was put in charge of a team of scientists to study UFO reports. It is no surprise that within weeks of his appointment he was quoted as saying: 'It is my inclination right now to recommend that the government get out of this business. My attitude right now is that there is nothing to it.'

The project, based at the University of Colorado, was something of a waste of tax-payers' money as very little serious and objective work was carried out into the UFO phenomenon. The general quality of the cases was poor. Condon focused on the wrong questions, as his final report made obvious. He asked if UFOs were indicative of visits by extraterrestrials rather than whether they represented an unknown phenomenon. When he could find no evidence for extraterrestrials, this allowed him to rubbish UFOs.

A split formed within the committee. One group of scientists who were more objective sent copies of a memo written by the university administrator, Robert Low, to other scientists working with civilian UFO groups. It was dated two months before the contract was awarded to the university, and sought to justify why they should have the work. Entitled 'Some Thoughts On The UFO Project', it said that the study 'would be conducted almost exclusively by non-believers', who 'could and probably would add an impressive body of evidence that there is no reality to the observations. The trick would be, I think, to describe the project so that, to the public, it would appear a totally objective study ...'

That suited the American government down to the ground. The conclusions of Condon were instrumental in Project Blue Book closing down in 1969, but many have since become convinced that it was nothing but a public relations white wash while the real UFO investigation went on in secret elsewhere.

Freedom of Information?
In 1976, the USA passed its Freedom of Information Act (FOIA) and Australia followed soon after. It would be naive in the extreme to believe that the American FOIA revealed the true extent of its government's interest in the UFO phenomenon. There was a get-out clause that meant files would only be released if they did not compromise national security.

Bruce Maccabee, a US Navy physicist, reported that during a conversation with Dr Christopher Green, who at one time was custodian of the CIA's UFO files, he admitted there were as many as 15,000 documents which had not been released into the public domain. However, the new law did allow public access to hitherto top secret documents that added substantially to our knowledge of the workings of the authorities during its decades of secret enquiry into alien activity.

The FBI, CIA and NSA fought tooth and nail against petitioners who rightly requested the release of thousands of documents. Initially, the National Security Agency denied having any files at all, then under pressure admitted to several hundred, but released just one, entitled 'UFO hypotheses and survival questions'. This suggested that the visitors *were* extraterrestrial.

Despite many appeals, they refused to release any more files. Protesters appealed to the Supreme Court, but even the top security-cleared judge presiding over the case was denied access to the files. Instead, the NSA gave him a twenty-one page document to read which detailed reasons *why* their UFO files had to be kept secret. When this was eventually released, ninety-five per cent of its content was blacked out. The judge agreed that release of the files would 'seriously jeopardise the work of the agency'.

The information which has been released revealed an administration which was intrigued and genuinely concerned by the UFO phenomenon. It did not have the tools to deal with it and publicly rubbished alien encounters while secretly admitting their reality. The

57

cover-up is probably as much to do with government impotence in the face of a superior intelligence than anything else. What is of little doubt is that the secret enquiry continues.

Despite the fact that the FBI claimed in a memo dated June 14, 1977, that it no longer investigated UFO-related phenomena, it has since emerged that the bureau was deeply involved in collating data on animal mutilations between 1974 and 1980. Thousands of head of cattle across the United States and Canada have been discovered drained of blood, with various organs surgically removed. UFOs were reported in the vicinity of many mutilations.

At late as 1988 the FBI were briefed on UFO sightings from China. There is every indication the authorities in America are as secretly involved in monitoring alien activity as ever.

Disinformation

There is also good evidence that the security services are not above sowing disinformation within the UFO community. What could be a prime example were documents anonymously sent to a handful of prominent ufologists in the late 1980s. The nine-page 'Top Secret' report – supposedly dated just after the Second World War – referred to a secret panel of politicians and scientists in the USA known as The Majestic Twelve, or MJ12.

According to the document, the twelve specialists were brought together to act as a think-tank on the UFO phenomenon in general and the Roswell case in particular. It included top nuclear scientist Dr Vannevar Bush, General Nathan Twining, who, according to other sources, had visited the Roswell crash site, and Rear-Admiral Roscoe Hillenkoetter, a director of the CIA and believer in the reality of UFOs. The MJ12 reported directly to President Truman.

It was Timothy Good who first went public with the document in 1987. Curiously, towards the end of the previous year, fellow researcher and author Jenny Randles and I were offered similar material under very strange circumstances.

Jenny received a telephone call from a man who claimed that his commanding officer in the British Army had asked him to release some classified documents into the UFO community. These comprised some six reports, totalling 600 pages. During the conversation certain names and codes were used by the man, which later tallied with the MJ12 documents. Included was a report from 1948, which contained the results of biological analyses of entities from UFO crashes, and another file dated October 1977, entitled 'Elimination of Non-Military Sources'.

Obviously, we wanted to get our hands on the files – if they existed. Eventually a meeting was arranged at a pub. Over several hours, 'John' gave a detailed account of the files and an elaborate but not unbelievable story of how he came into possession of them. His replies to our hard questioning were detailed and confident. If the whole incident was a hoax, he had been very well briefed and possessed the acting ability to carry it off.

According to our informant, his commanding officer spent time serving in the USA, where he befriended an American at Wright-Patterson Air Force Base. This man accidentally accessed some computer files on UFOs and copied them before being arrested. His British friend smuggled them into England, as both men believed they should be released into the public domain. The American then died in a car crash, which his friend thought was murder.

John's commanding officer wondered what was the safest way to release the papers and decided he needed a confederate. It was only when John left the Army and returned at weekends for reservist training that he decided to enlist his help after months of subtle questioning to ensure he was sympathetic. At this stage he told John the story, and informed him where the files were hidden and who to contact. Hence the meeting with us in a quiet corner of a smoky pub near Manchester. As we listened to him and asked questions veering on the side of scepticism, the whole encounter had a surreal feel to it.

Of course, we wanted proof, but John did not have the documents on him that day. He claimed they were split up into batches and hidden in various places. After speaking to us, he agreed that we could see a sample of the material before deciding whether to hand over the lot. A second meeting was arranged at a country park near Warrington, but John never turned up, so we wrote the whole episode off as an elaborate hoax. However, the story had a curious twist.

Ten days later Jenny Randles received a letter from John in which he apologised for not attending the meeting, but explained that at the time he was the subject of an internal investigation by the Army. He claimed that two days after seeing us, he was taken to his base and interrogated about 'sensitive' documents. These were 'the creation of an educated prankster' to which 'no credence could be attributed'.

We never heard from John again. How papers could be 'sensitive' when they contained nothing of credence is hard to see. However, the release of the MJ12 documents convinced us that John was not a lone hoaxer acting on his own initiative – if he was a hoaxer at all. Perhaps he was being conned, too? It all tied in somehow with a disinformation campaign that was being targeted at the UFO community.

However, not everyone believes that. Another prominent ufologist to whom the papers were sent was nuclear physicist Stanton Friedman. To this day he is convinced of their authenticity. Central to his argument is the signature of President Harry Truman, which appears on the document. Friedman, and others, point out that it is *identical* to Truman's signature as seen on another non-UFO paper. I would have thought this works against authenticity. No one signs their signature in *exactly* the same way twice.

What would be the purpose of releasing bogus documents like MJ12? That is a difficult question to answer. It all depends on who was behind it. Perhaps the intelligence community are trying to shape our beliefs by introducing the odd red herring into the equation. They might want us to go on thinking that extraterrestrials lie behind the UFO phenomenon when the real answer could be even stranger ...

4

The Secret Inquiry in Britain

Without a viable Freedom of Information Act, it is more difficult in Britain to get a feel for the true extent of the secret enquiry into UFOs by our government. While one is promised for the near future, the proposals are so watered down it will be nothing more than a cosmetic exercise. Indeed it has been dubbed a Freedom *From* Information Act. Despite a lack of legislation, we know from American documentation that the British kept in regular contact with their counterparts in the USA, who were carrying out research and investigation into the phenomenon.

Ironically, it is through the American FOIA that we know of Britain's input into ATIC's controversial 'Estimate of the Situation' report, which contained details of English 'ghost airplanes'. It was also through the FOIA that researchers in Britain were able to obtain the report by Colonel Charles Halt of a close encounter in Rendlesham Forest, Suffolk, in December 1980, originally submitted to our Ministry of Defence. Britain has the thirty-year rule, after which sensitive documents can be released into the archives of the Public Record Office in London, but this is not mandatory, and data can be withheld for fifty or a hundred years.

What is not in doubt is that the British military became concerned about UFOs at around the same time as the Americans. They already had on record some good quality sightings which predated the famous 1947 Kenneth Arnold event. But it was during a NATO exercise over the North Sea and North Atlantic Ocean in September 1952 that Britain's interest in UFOs was reinforced.

Operation Mainbrace

Dubbed 'Mainbrace', it involved the military forces of the USA, Britain, Canada, France, Belgium, Norway, Denmark and the Netherlands. The purpose of Mainbrace was to deter the Soviet Union from launching an attack on Western Europe. But it seemed that some other power apart from the Russians was taking a keen interest in the operation.

Just one day into the exercise, ships in the Atlantic reported a 'blue/green triangle' flying over the sea at 1,500 mph. In a separate incident, three objects emitting a 'white light exhaust' in a triangular formation were observed travelling at a similar speed. On September 19, personnel belonging to 269 Squadron based at RAF Topcliffe in Yorkshire were witness to an extraordinary sighting. The following day a report was submitted by Flight Lieutenant John Kilburn on behalf of himself and four other air crew.

Kilburn described how he, Flying Officer R. N. Paris, Flight Lieutenant M. Cybulski, Master Sergeant Thompson, Sergeant Dewis and Leading Aircraftsman Grimes were watching a Meteor fighter gradually descending in sunlit clear sky conditions with 'unlimited visibility'. Paris drew their attention to an object 'silver in colour and circular in shape' higher than the aircraft and about five miles astern, on a similar course.

After a few seconds, it began to descend, 'swinging in a pendular motion similar to a falling sycamore leaf'. This manoeuvre was a feature of many UFO sightings until the mid-1970s. The men tried to rationalise the experience by speculating that the object might be a parachute or an engine cowling. They quickly realised this could not be the case when the object stopped its motion and began rotating about its axis.

Suddenly, it accelerated in a westerly direction, turned south-easterly, then disappeared from sight. Kilburn told his superiors: 'The movements of the object were not identifiable with anything I have seen in the air. The rate of acceleration was unbelievable.' Copies of the report were sent to a NATO Commander-in-Chief and a number of British government departments.

The following day, the USS aircraft carrier *Franklin D. Roosevelt* was involved in a close encounter. Press photographer Wallace Litwin was on board to take pictures during the exercise when he saw a circular, silver coloured object above the ship. He managed to take three colour shots of the UFO with the *Roosevelt* in the frame. Researcher Nic Redfern, who has seen the photographs, comments that although they are not of 'exceptional quality', they *do* show a circular object.

Just twenty-four hours later, an object of the same description was seen over the North Sea. A number of RAF fighters attempted to intercept the UFO, but it easily out paced them. Objects were also recorded on radar, and the tapes confiscated.

Despite sightings of this calibre made by trained military observers and recorded on radar, like the Americans, the British government has always sought to down play UFOs. The result is a sort of double-think foisted on the general public, and perhaps even a Premier!

In July 1952, Prime Minister Winston Churchill wrote to the Secretary of State for Air demanding to know the 'truth' behind 'flying saucers'. A month later, the Air Ministry announced that its 'full intelligence study' had concluded that *all* UFO incidents could be attributed to astronomical phenomena, misidentification of man-made aerial objects, optical illusions and hoaxes.

One of the architects behind this white-wash was R. G. Woodman, Deputy Superintendent of Test Flying at Boscombe Down. He drew his conclusions after examining UFO reports made by air crews of the RAF and the Royal Navy. It does not say much for our military personnel's powers of observation! Ironically, just months after the publication of the Air Ministry's report, a mid-air collision with a daylight disc was only just avoided in Woodman's own backyard, the air space above Boscombe Down, involving test crew under his command.

Head-On Collision - Almost!

Flight Lieutenant Cyril George Townsend-Withers prepared to carry out tests on a new airborne radar system one crisp, sunny winter's day in 1953. The equipment was installed in a Canberra aircraft stripped bare of non-essential equipment to enable the aircraft to be as light as possible. Once everything was ready, the Canberra took off from Boscombe Down carrying Lieutenant Townsend-Withers and his pilot. As it soared to 55,000 feet – a record for the Canberra – it encountered another aircraft 'not of this world', as Townsend-Withers was to tell Jenny Randles and me in 1986.

Now retired, the affable, grey haired man waited more than thirty years to ensure some protection from possible prosecution. Even so, Townsend-Withers was not absolutely sure he should speak of the incident, but needed to tell someone, and had waited long enough. We had no doubts he was telling the truth.

As the aircraft cruised over Salisbury Plain just after noon, Townsend-Withers picked up an unidentifiable blip on the radar screen. It showed that an object was apparently tailing them some five miles distant. Initially, he put it down to anomalous propagation which had caused problems with the equipment previously, but climbed up into the turret and obtained visual confirmation that there was indeed an object following them.

From that distance, it looked like a bright sphere which was either reflecting the sunlight or pouring out light of its own. He informed the pilot and suggested they try and out-run the object. They reached 225 knots, but the UFO kept pace. The pilot then executed a U-turn, which effectively put it on a collision course with the unknown object. It was dead ahead and drawing closer, giving the men an excellent view. They could now see it was disc-shaped and metallic looking, with two tail fins about the size of a Gnat fighter. As the men speculated on what to do next, the decision was abruptly taken out of their hands as the object suddenly shot upwards out of harm's way at an astonishing speed.

'Fifty, sixty, seventy thousand feet – as quick as you could say it,' Townsend-Withers explained to us, still spellbound, his eyes blue and staring through us, reaching back there, a lifetime ago. The object was gone after a few seconds, leaving no vapour trail, sound or wake. Gone. Faster than anything the young RAF officer had ever seen. He felt it acted like 'a reconnaissance device from somewhere else'.

After the aircraft landed safely, the two men decided to make an official report. They were debriefed, but astonished by the reactions of the officers making the report. 'Once we satisfied them it was not a Russian plane, they were just not interested.' The report was passed to the Air Ministry, who told Townsend-Withers they were evaluating UFO sightings from the point of view they might be inter-planetary. He never heard from them again.

Despite Woodman's belief that *all* UFOs had a mundane expla-nation, Townsend-Withers' experience did him no harm, consid-ering that, according to the 'full intelligence study', he must have misidentified a natural phenomenon or hoaxed the incident. Cyril George Townsend-Withers was later promoted to Senior Scientific

Officer and attained the rank of Wing Commander. One could be forgiven for thinking that the phenomenon was sticking up two fingers at R. G. Woodman.

Official Reactions

While trying to explain away every UFO sighting, one wonders who the authorities were really trying to kid. Certainly Members of Parliament and the public whom they represent were prime targets. The same year that Townsend-Withers and his pilot had their encounter, Flying Officers Geoffrey Smythe and Terry Johnson reported a round, bright object observed while they were flying at around 20,000 feet. After watching it for thirty seconds it suddenly accelerated away at a terrific rate.

Both men were questioned for two hours by Air Ministry officials, who obviously took their sighting very seriously. When MPs demanded to know more, the Parliamentary Secretary to the Air Ministry informed the House of Commons that the pilots had mistaken a weather balloon.

While not doubting that balloons of all types and sizes do account for some UFO sightings, it has been a convenient 'explanation' to throw at a problem that defies all logic. When a number of people in Wardle, Lancashire, sighted an aerial object in February 1957 it gained sufficient publicity for questions to be raised in the House of Commons. Charles Orr-Ewing, Under-Secretary of State for Air, told the House the witnesses had fallen victim to a hoax involving two toy balloons filled with hydrogen perpetrated by a laundry mechanic.

In 1989, the editor of the *Heywood Advertiser* recalled the case, which he investigated thirty-two years earlier as a young reporter. Then he had interviewed the laundry man, who was unable to explain from where he obtained the hydrogen for the balloons, and as good as admitted that his claim for hoaxing the sighting was a hoax itself. The newspaper reported all of this at the time, whereupon they were visited by an official from the Ministry of Defence. According to the editor, he 'took us into a private back room and read the Official Secrets Act to us with the warning to discontinue reporting further on that strange occurrence'.

On December 16, 1953, a document entitled 'Reports on Aerial Phenomena' was prepared by the Air Ministry for circulation within the RAF. It was designed to promote the correct procedures to submit UFO reports, and to ensure the ministry controlled the release of data to the British public. All reports were to be classified 'Restricted' and personnel warned not to discuss their sightings unless officially authorised to do so.

In 1956, this was upgraded to 'Secret'. This, of course, reveals the lie that all UFOs had mundane explanations otherwise why bother covering anything up? Indeed, on May 15, 1957, the Secretary of State for Air, George Ward, admitted to MPs that there were six UFO reports from 1954 for which they were unable to find an explanation. Another UFO incident Ward could have added to that list occurred two years later.

The Lakenheath Encounter

The event involved ground personnel and fighter aircraft from the joint RAF/USAF bases near Sculthorpe, Norfolk, Lakenheath and Bentwaters in Suffolk, and the RAF command centre in Norfolk at Neatishead. It was through a report which surfaced in America that details emerged: the British MoD had always maintained they have no files on the case. It began early in the evening of August 13, 1956, when radar at all four bases tracked an object after a USAF transport aircraft flying at 5,000 feet reported that a blurred light had passed beneath it.

Squadron Leader Freddy Wimbledon ordered two Venom fighters into the area. They picked up the object on their radars. According to Wimbleton, who waited thirty years to tell his story, a hide-and-seek game ensued, with the UFO at one point sweeping around to position itself behind one of the fighters. Jenny Randles says she has traced civilians in Cambridgeshire who saw the bright object tailing behind the aircraft. Squadron Leader Wimbledon also claims that the air crew had visual confirmation of the object. In a report made to the Condon Committee, the Watch Supervisor in the radar centre at Lakenheath supports the story. Here is a condensed version of his statement:

> They [Sculthorpe] said they had watched a target on their scopes [and] the tower reported seeing it go by and [it] just appeared to be a blurry light. I immediately had all the

controllers start scanning the radar scopes. One controller noticed a stationary target about 20 to 25 miles south-west. As we watched [it] started moving at a speed of 400 to 600 mph. There was no slow build-up to this speed – it was constant from the second it started to move until it stopped. The target made several changes in location, always in a straight line, always at about 600 mph and always from a standing or stationary point. After about 30 to 45 minutes, it was decided to scramble two RAF interceptors. They scrambled one aircraft – the second got off after. We immediately issued heading to the interceptor to guide him to the UFO. Shortly after we told the intercept aircraft he was one-half mile from the UFO, he said, "Roger, Lakenheath, I've got my guns locked on him." Then he paused and said: "Where did he go? Do you still have him?" We replied: "Roger. It appeared he got behind you and he's still there."

He tried everything [to shake the UFO off] – he climbed, dived, circled, but the UFO acted like glue. The interceptor pilot continued to try and shake the UFO for about ten minutes. We could tell from the tonal quality he was getting worried, excited and also pretty scared. He finally said: "I'm returning to station, Lakenheath. Let me know if he follows me." The target followed him only a short distance, stopped and remained stationary. He rogered this message, and almost immediately the second interceptor called us on the same frequency.

The number-two interceptor called the number-one interceptor and asked him, "Did you see anything?" Number-one replied, "I saw something, but I'll be damned if I know what it was." We gave number-two the location of the UFO. He delayed answering for some seconds and then finally said: "Lakenheath, returning home. My engine is malfunctioning." The target made a couple more short moves, then left our radar coverage in a northerly direction.

This statement was made more than ten years after the incident, and some of the details have been challenged. For instance, according to Jenny Randles, the second interceptor did not return because of engine trouble. If there *was* mechanical problems that would tie in with other cases where the electrical systems of aircraft and motor vehicles have been affected during close encounters with UFOs.

In February 1996, Jenny Randles spoke to one of the pilots and the navigators of both RAF Venoms. Strangely, none of them recounts having a visual sighting of the object, despite claims to the contrary. Of course, it could have been the second pilot, but he emigrated to South Africa and his whereabouts are unknown. Despite these minor problems, the case was a major step in the escalation of alien activity.

UFOs And Military Installations

In the wake of Lakenheath, a number of UFO incidents occurred around military installations, as files formerly classified 'Secret' reveal. On March 26, 1957, the RAF base at Church Lawford plotted an object on radar which accelerated from a standing position to a speed of 1400 mph. RAF West Freugh, Wigtownshire, was next visited on April 4. Radar operators picked up a stationary object which began to move off after ten minutes, and then made a sharp turn. The echo was larger than that of a normal aircraft, and more like that expected from a ship. Four smaller objects appeared. All then went out of range.

The official report said that the objects, tracked by three radars, attained an altitude of 70,000 feet and a speed of 240 mph. It concluded 'that the incident was due to the presence of five reflecting objects of unidentified type and origin. It is considered unlikely that they were conventional aircraft, meteorological balloons or charged clouds.'

On August 13, 1960, Ernest Sears, who formerly served with the RAF, was walking through Gosport when he noticed a 'glowing cigar' hovering above the Air Surface Weapons Establishment on Portsdown Hill. Thirty minutes later two Meteor jets came low over the rooftops and climbed up towards the object, which had not moved. As the aircraft closed in, the UFO turned on end then disappeared 'like somebody switching a light bulb out'.

When Sears telephoned Thorney Island aerodrome and asked about the incident he was told: 'You didn't see any object. Neither did you see jets.' Sears persisted, but the official just repeated what he had already said. At that time, Sears' brother-in-law worked at the Air Surface Weapons Establishment as an electrical draughtsman. The following night when Sears tackled him about the encounter, the man 'went white and his mouth set in a grim line'.

Government Investigations

It was not until April 1, 1964, that the Air Ministry, War Office and the Admiralty were unified into the Ministry of Defence. UFO reports were dealt with by two departments. DS8 was one of them. A former head, the late Ralph Noyes, claimed after his retirement to have seen gun camera film of UFOs. According to some sources, the serious work of UFO investigation was carried out by members of a new division called Defence Intelligence Staff, operating out of RAF Farnborough.

In the late 1980s, writer Tim Good added that investigations were also carried out by agents of the Provost and Security Services from RAF Rudloe Manor. There was some verification in 1995 when MoD spokeswomen Kerry Philpott told researcher Chris Fowler that the base 'was indeed the co-ordination point for reports of "unexplained" aerial sightings'.

The responsibility for collating UFO reports from the general public was moved from Department Secretariat 8 to Secretariat (Air Staff) 2a. In 1991, Nic Pope became the Desk Officer, serving until 1994. Mr Pope was UFO-friendly, and seemed to go out of his way to assist civilian organisations, and indeed courted several leading investigators. He appeared to have a genuine interest in the subject and a real desire to help, but was there a hidden agenda, too?

When it was announced that Pope was going to bring out his own book on UFOs, everyone held their breath – naively perhaps – believing it would contain some hitherto unpublished material from the secret MoD archives. However, ufologists were disappointed. Despite the media hype, *Open Skies Closed Minds* and its follow-up *Abduction* contained mainly material that was already in the public domain. The media dubbed Pope the 'MoD's UFO expert'. He fell easily into that role.

For his book *A Covert Agenda*, Nic Redfern interviewed Pope regarding UFO investigation within the MoD. While Redfern applauded Pope for his honesty and co-operation, he had doubts about how much he actually knew. Pope told him that Sec (AS) 2a had no appreciable budget to investigate UFOs, yet Tim Good claims that £11 million were appropriated by the MoD in 1978. Where had the money gone? Redfern concludes that Sec (AS) 2a actually fulfils a very minor role in the MoD's programme of UFO study.

Considering that publicly UFOs are rubbished by the authorities it is strange they have in place procedures for reporting what they would have us believe is a non-existent phenomenon. When a member of the public makes a report to a police station, officers fill in a form and send it to the MoD. The Civil Aviation Authority are particularly instructed on how to deal with UFOs in their 'Manual of Air Traffic Services'. This states: 'A controller receiving a report about an unidentified object must obtain as much as possible of the information required to complete a report. The report is to be sent by the originating air traffic service unit to the Ministry of Defence.'

In October 1988 a surprising admission was made by Flight Sergeant Dave Pengilly from RAF Brawdy in Pembrokeshire. He interviewed a Mr and Mrs Silvestri who lived in Cilau Aeron, Wales, after 'a brilliant greenish light' lit up the interior of their car. According to the couple, the Flight Sergeant told them: 'Each report of this kind is always investigated. I make checks and then pass it on to the powers-that-be in the Ministry of Defence. We don't like unidentified things in our airspace.' That flies in the face of the usual stock statement from the MoD that they are not interested in UFOs because they 'have no defence implications'.

It would seem that the authorities are not beyond manufacturing an explanation to diffuse public and media interest in a case, as investigator Tony Dodd discovered. When residents in Sowerby Bridge, Yorkshire, reported seeing a large disc-shaped object near Scammonden Reservoir in the early evening of November 2, 1995, Dodd investigated. The witnesses also claimed that around seven aircraft and three helicopters had circled around the UFO before it disappeared.

Interestingly, RAF West Drayton admitted they knew about the event, although their interpretation did not exactly gel with that of the civilian witnesses. The authorities told Dodd that there had been a military exercise which caused floodlights around the reservoir to explode. However, when he pursued the matter, Yorkshire Water told him that no floodlights had been damaged!

By now it must be obvious that the British, like the Americans, have been conducting intense research into the UFO subject. The accounts by pilots and other professional observers do not tally with the official statements put out by government departments to white-wash the subject. They know, like us, that something strange and awesome is going on – right under our noses.

5

The Secret Inquiry Elsewhere

The Canadian Experience

The Canadian authorities have also had an ambiguous attitude towards the subject of UFOs. One minute they have embraced the reality of alien activity, and then gone into denial. For instance, in March 1971 the Department of External Affairs told ufologist Arthur Bray: 'The Canadian Government does not underestimate the seriousness of the question of UFOs. This matter is kept under consideration and study in a number of departments and agencies.' Yet just six years later, Transport Canada, responsible for air safety, flatly denied knowledge of any instances of intrusions by UFOs into Canadian air space. This was an amazing statement considering the existence of several well-attested cases of close encounters between civil aircraft and unidentified objects.

Project Magnet was the Canadian government's first investigation into UFOs, established in 1950 under the direction of Senior Radio Engineer Wilbert B. Smith. Magnet had a small budget using Department of Transport facilities with help from the Defence Research Board and National Research Council. Smith's team included three engineers and two technicians. It was many years before details of this classified project seeped into the public domain.

Smith was already involved in research into geomagnetism as a possible source of new energy. At that time, some scientists believed that UFOs operated on magnetic principles so it made sense to Smith that a study of this phenomenon might help his investigation. He made a proposal to the Deputy Minister of Transport for Air Services, Commander C. P. Edwards, who gave his formal approval.

In tandem with Project Magnet, a separate committee was formed, code-named Project Second Storey. Apart from Smith, the committee comprised a number of scientists and military officers whose job it was to meet and consider the UFO problem and advise the Canadian government accordingly.

Smith's research was in two parts. The first involved collating as many good quality reports as possible and analysing them. Then he intended examining the results minutely to see if there were any clues to a new technology.

In November 1953 Project Magnet installed some sophisticated recording equipment in a station situated at Shirley's Bay, near Ottawa. On August 8, 1954, the instruments went wild, recording an electromagnetic disturbance by something which had passed relatively close to the station. This was totally different to disturbances registered from terrestrial aircraft, but misty low level cloud conditions prevented a visual sighting.

Two days later the Department of Transport announced they were scrapping Project Magnet. Smith carried on at his own expense and in his own time. Was the project dropped because it was too successful? In official reports, Wilbert Smith made the following observations concerning his research into UFOs:

> During the past five years, there has been accumulating an impressive number of reports on sightings of unidentified flying objects. These files contain reports by credible people on things they have seen in the sky, tracked by radar, or photographed. Many sightings undoubtedly are due to unusual views of common objects or phenomena, but there are many which cannot be explained so easily.
>
> It has been suggested that the sightings might be due to some sort of optical phenomenon which gives the appearance of objects, and this aspect was thoroughly investigated. It appears that we are faced with a substantial probability of the real existence of extraterrestrial vehicles, regardless of whether or not they fit into our scheme of things. Such vehicles of necessity must use a technology considerably in advance of what we have.

Back In The USSR

Since the thaw of the Cold War and the collapse of the Russian empire, high-ranking military personnel have been very forthcoming regarding official Soviet attitudes and investigations into UFOs. Indeed, they are more outspoken than their western counterparts and readily embrace the fact that behind the UFO phenomenon lies an alien intelligence.

Valeriy Burdakov, a scientist who worked at the Moscow Aviation Institute in the 1950s, told two American researchers during a visit to Russia in 1993 that when he confided his interest in UFOs to Sergei Korolyov, founder of the Soviet space programme, the man told him an amazing story.

Korolyov claimed he had been invited to a meeting with Josef Stalin in 1948. There, Stalin asked for his opinion of a wealth of material collated during a top secret study of the UFO phenomenon. After examining the material, Korolyov told the Soviet leader that the phenomenon was real, and that it did not originate in the United States or in any other country.

Astonishingly, despite the fact that Britain and the Soviet Union were sworn enemies, in 1967 it was being suggested in government circles that the two powers conduct a joint UFO study programme. Does this mean that UFOs were perceived as being above the petty differences of East and West, presenting a global threat to all mankind?

The suggestion came about when it was announced on Soviet television in early November that Russia had set up a commission to study UFOs under the chairmanship of Major General A. F. Stolyarov, a former Technical Services Officer with the Soviet Air Force. Initially, when a Reuters correspondent tried to pursue the story it was confirmed, but two months later came a report that the commission had been disbanded because of insufficient information to sustain it. However, in the meantime, it attracted the attentions of the British government.

As a document released by the US Defence Intelligence Agency clearly shows that on December 12 the British Embassy was ordered to approach the Russians with a view 'to co-operate in observation teams for UFOs'. The embassy's Scientific Counsellor met the State Committee for Science and Technology and put the suggestion to them. They promised to get back to him regarding the proposal. This did not happen, however. Then came the announcement that the project had been scrapped.

It was the view of the Scientific Counsellor that the commission's original announcement was a mistake on the part of the Soviet censor, and that it had not been disbanded, but was continuing undercover. This is highly likely since according to computer scientist Dr Jacques Vallee, by the mid-1960s over ten thousand close encounter cases had been logged by the Soviets. In 1984 a team of military investigators was mounted to look into sightings, headed by cosmonaut Marina Popovich. Then on October 9, 1989, something unprecedented happened – Tass, the Soviet news agency, announced to the world that a UFO had landed in the USSR and aliens been observed nearby!

The Voronezh Aliens

I was as astonished as everyone else at this new openness by the Russians. The story featured in all the media for days, and caused a lot of debate and controversy. It seemed that one of the main investigators was Dr Henry Silanov, Director of the Spectral Department of the Voronezh Geological-Geophysical Laboratory, the industrial town where the incidents happened. I wrote to Dr Silanov asking for details of the affair, and was pleasantly surprised to receive a personal letter and his report, which included the testimonies of several witnesses. This is what Dr Silanov told me:

> In the period between September 21 to October 28, in the Western Park, six landings and one sighting (hovering) were registered, with the appearances of walking beings. We have collected a wealth of video material with eye-witness accounts, particularly from pupils of the nearest school. We have no doubts that they are telling the truth because details of the landings and other signs are recounted by the children who could otherwise only have got this information from specialist UFO literature, which is not publicised in this country.

The accounts Dr Silanov sent me were from some of the students. This is Vasya Surin's story:

> It was a few days after I had come out of hospital on September 19. We were playing football in the park during

the evening as it was just getting dark. Then we saw from the direction of the [untranslatable name of building] first a sort of pink haze, as if someone had lit a bonfire in fog. This haze was higher in the sky than the chimney stack of the building. Then we told everyone who was around, and they stopped to watch. From the middle of the fog appeared a sort of red sphere. The fog did not move. It stood still, but the sphere flew away at great speed.

It stopped over a tree, then lowered slightly on to the top of the tree, rested on it and the tree bowed under it. We got frightened: we thought they might see us if we ran home and might take us away. Then we hid in the bushes and kept watch.

A door opened in the sphere [and] a person (being) looked out. He was tall – about three metres – shone silvery, and his arms were down to his knees. He stood up, looked around, but could not move his head. It was as if he didn't have one, as if it was just a continuation of his shoulders. [There were] three eyes – two at the sides, and a third just a little higher, which moved up and down, left and right. They started to climb down the tree, first a robot and then an extraterrestrial. The robot had no head. [The] extraterrestrial walked up to the robot and seemed to punch out some numbers to enter a code on the robot's chest, and it started to walk mechanically.

It walked along the road a bit, while the extraterrestrial said something and a rectangle appeared on the ground. The rectangle was red and you could see lights in it. Then he spoke again and all this disappeared. One of the little boys who hadn't managed to hide shouted out in fright. The extraterrestrial looked at him and the boy seemed rooted to the spot. When the extraterrestrial looked at him, his side-eyes seemed to light up. Only when he stopped looking, did the boy move a little.

A young man was walking along the road, perhaps to the bus stop. The extraterrestrial noticed him, climbed up the tree into the sphere and came out with something like a pistol, yellow with a telescopic sight. The young man, when he saw the alien, ran off, and the latter aimed the pistol at him and he disappeared. The robot walked up to the extraterrestrial, who said something to it before climbing the tree back into the sphere, whereupon it flew away. As soon as it was gone, the man reappeared and carried on walking as if he had seen nothing!

One evening towards the end of September, just after 7 pm a young man called Denis Valyerervich Murzenko changed his clothes to accompany his mother to a concert and discovered he had some time on his hands, so decided to take a walk. Looking up into the sky, he saw something pink, shaped like an egg, with rays of light coming from it. The object came closer and began to swing from side to side and lose height in the familiar falling leaf motion featured in some earlier western cases. At this juncture, two supports came out from underneath. Denis noticed a symbol painted on it which resembled a Russian letter. Now the object was close enough for him to make out the features of a being sitting inside:

> The 'person' seemed to be about one-and-a-half metres high, with an old face. I stood still and it kept coming down, lower and lower. I became frightened and ran off. When I turned, I saw bright beams of light. There was some kind of sound like music.

There were several young witnesses to another incident which happened at around 2.30 pm on October 28. The children were playing truant from school when they saw a large pink sphere overhead with the same curious symbol on it. Here is the statement of one of them, Vova Startsev:

> It was flying quite low. It passed the street lights and landed here. It was pink, but kept changing shade. On the left hand side were two antennae. It pushed out four legs, a hatch opened, a ladder came down and two beings and a robot came out. They carried the robot, set him on his feet, gave him artificial respiration, then he walked like a man.

It came up to me, followed by one of the extraterrestrials. He was just under two metres tall, stretched out his hand towards me, but I ran towards a tree and climbed it, shaking with fear. The alien had a big head, twice as big as ours, and three eyes in a row.

Another of the boys, Sergei Makarov, described the aliens as wearing silver suits, with silver waistcoats, buttons and boots to match. Their faces were the colour of 'grilled beefburgers', but smooth looking. He said that when the door to the object opened it emitted a blinding light, which prevented them from seeing any interior details. The boys recalled how the legs retracted and the object hovered before taking off.

The witnesses were aged between thirteen and sixteen: adults were hard to find. Was this because older Soviet citizens had an ingrained fear of voicing things which the State might judge to be subversive? One adult who did back up the claims of the students was Sergei Matveyev, a lieutenant in the local militia. He saw 'an object almost fifteen metres in diameter over the park' that same night when Vasya Surin and his friends had their encounter.

Dr Silanov claimed that a site analysis found 'incredibly high levels of magnetism'. He was further quoted as saying, 'It is evident that something produced it.' That 'something' left imprints in the ground which his laboratory assistants concluded would have required a pressure of eleven tonnes. Ludmilla Makarova, a spokesperson for the local militia investigation unit, commented that there was 'abnormally high radio-activity' in the park. It was strongest inside the impressions.

When I attempted to obtain further information from Dr Silanov, my letters were unanswered.

Australia, Spain and France

Perhaps learning from the American experience, the Australian government decided to dispense its secret UFO files through one man rather than deal with multiple applications from various groups and individuals. They invited respected ufologist Bill Chalker to extract and copy the released data. Chalker did a first class job disseminating the information around the UFO community. What became clear, however, was that the authorities in Australia were just as confused as their counterparts in the USA. While most UFO encounters had a rational explanation, there was a hard-core of water-tight cases that had 'alien' ramifications.

Files released in France and Spain during the 1980s and 1990s reveal a similar picture. In 1976, journalist Jose Benitez was invited to Madrid by the Chief of Staff to the Air Ministry, and handed documentation on twelve military cases, including gun camera film of UFOs. Since then details of radar trackings, aerial encounters and unsolved sightings have been released from time to time by the Spanish authorities.

France had its own 'Project Blue Book', GEPAN, staffed by open-minded scientists rather than individuals 'owned' by the military and secret services. The way was cleared for the Study Group into Unidentified Aerospatial Phenomena (as it translates) after an admission by the French government of the reality of UFOs. In March 1974, the Minister of Defence, Robert Galley, went on national radio and reported that Air Force jets had chased UFOs on many occasions, and that the extent and depth of the cases were very disturbing. Not surprisingly, the British media totally ignored this historic statement.

GEPAN was launched on May 1, 1977, under the directorship of Dr Claude Poher from the French Space Agency at Toulouse. The *gendarmerie* were trained to follow up reports and bring in GEPAN should they think it necessary. A number of laboratories were on standby to carry out analyses of ground traces or any other material associated with an alien encounter.

During 1978 three hundred and fifty four reports were sent to GEPAN, and over 1,600 in 1985. More than fifty per cent of these represented close encounters, as the police had already filtered out the more mundane lights in the sky which were likely to have a rational explanation. GEPAN evaluated a quarter of the reports as genuine encounters with something anomalous. The scientists were very excited by their findings and just two years into the project applied for more government funding. This was successful, but it came with strings. More funding meant more government control and more secrecy. Those holding the purse-strings were disconcerted by the hard physical evidence for UFOs and cautioned 'great vigilance' in what was released for public consumption.

Dr Poher was replaced by a young astronomer, Dr Alain Esterle, who was not as open as his predecessor. Nevertheless, he intimated to British ufologist Jenny Randles in May 1981 that his team of scientists were coming round to the conclusion that some of the evidence supported the hypothesis that an alien intelligence lay behind the phenomenon. However, in 1983 Dr Pierre Guerin, who had been involved with GEPAN since its inception, went public with a statement that the authorities were trying to persuade the team 'to deny the existence of UFOs' and therefore defuse interest. They particularly wanted to target the wider scientific community in this way. In essence, factions within the French government were trying to use GEPAN as the American secret services did with Blue Book. GEPAN was to be a tool to rubbish the UFO subject.

In the late 1980s, GEPAN, now called SEPRA to take into account its expanded role of investigating the re-entry of space junk, basically went underground. Right up to the 1990s, whenever the media and respected ufologists tried to obtain information from SEPRA on UFO sightings, they were met with silence.

Hard Evidence at Trans-en-Provence?
One of the most celebrated cases which involved GEPAN was an alleged landing of a UFO at Trans-en-Provence. This area of south-eastern France had long been a focus for UFO activity, so when the *gendarmerie* received a new report, they took it in their stride. However, there was something different about this case, for the witness described a *landing*.

Farmer Renato Nicolai lived in the slope of a valley above a series of terraced orchards leading down to the River Nartuby. At around 5 pm on January 8, 1981, he was working in the orchard when he heard a 'faint whistling' and turned to see 'a device in the air at the height of a big pine tree ... not spinning, coming lower towards the ground'.

The object was slightly smaller than a car and shaped like an elongated egg, with four circular openings at the base. Renato said it was 'the colour of lead' and that 'the device had a ridge around its circumference'. The farmer thought that two of the openings 'could be reactors or feet'. There were also two other circles, which looked like 'trap-doors'. He noticed two small legs at the base.

Renato walked towards the object, which had now touched down on the slope. But 'right away it lifted off, still emitting a slight whistling sound, kicking off a little dust when it left'. After the object climbed twenty feet it sped off in a north-easterly direction.

When the police investigated, they discovered there was more to it than just the farmer's story. Apparently, the UFO left proof of its visit – a ring in the earth several centimetres wide and two metres in diameter. GEPAN were contacted and instructed the police to take samples from the area of the ring, and control samples from some distance away.

The analyses was carried out at the National Institute for Agronomy Research by Michael Bounais, an expert in fauna damage. There were some remarkable findings. The chlorophyll content of plants from the ring was different from those outside it. Also the grass had aged 'in some way that neither natural processes nor laboratory experiments could duplicate'. The ground, too, in the area of the ring had suffered major deformations. In conclusion, GEPAN said: 'We cannot give any precise or specific interpretation for this remarkable set of results ... But we can state that there is nevertheless confirmation that a very significant incident took place.'

This caused GEPAN director Alain Esterle to enthuse, 'We have a combination of factors which induce us to accept that something akin to what the witness described actually did take place.' Esterle's successor, Jean Jacques Velasco, thought that an electromagnetic field rather than irradiating energy was more likely to have been responsible for the plant and soil changes. In 1990, Bounais published an article in the *Journal of Scientific Exploration* in which he admitted his bafflement because neither ionisation, thermal nor hydro factors could have been responsible for the changes.

However, ufologist Jacques Scornaux has been very critical of the investigation. He noted inconsistencies in the farmer's report and believes the police officers did not collect the soil samples as they were ordered, giving misleading results. Dr Jacques Vallee visited the site in November 1988 and took away samples for analysis at a laboratory in California. The scientists there, who wished to remain anonymous, were as baffled as their French colleagues.

GEPAN carried out a first class investigation into the landing at Trans-en-Provence, the results of which were in the public domain. Perhaps they did too good a job because it was not long after that GEPAN/SEPRA went underground.

It must be apparent by now that governments around the world have sought to diffuse public interest in the UFO phenomenon by claiming that it does not exist. While they are doing this on the one hand, on the other they are carrying out long term investigation and study into the subject.

There is no doubt that there has been a cover-up by those in charge. I believe the reason for that subterfuge has more to do with their own confusion than a desire to hide from the public the true origins of the phenomenon. The aliens, whatever they turn out to be, and wherever they originate from, are undoubtedly here.

6

A Dangerous Liaison

The evidence for alien activity lies on many different levels. On one rests a large body of historical records going back to ancient times describing contact between man and beings from other worlds. Then there are the covert investigations into UFOs by military and government security departments. The contents of many of their files are startling.

On a one-to-one basis we have witnesses, many of whom are beyond reproach, including pilots, police officers, scientists and politicians. They have a lot to lose by making public their sightings and experiences. More interesting are multiple witness events, which are harder to explain away in terms of misidentification or hallucination. Finally, there is the physical proof of aliens, which includes changes or damage to the environment, film and photographic evidence, radar traces, electromagnetic effects on aircraft and land vehicles, and damage to biological systems. By that I mean the psychological and physiological alterations incurred by humans and animals who have come into contact with the visitors. In many cases these prove fatal.

Over the years I have interviewed hundreds of people left distraught by contact with the phenomenon. Many held responsible jobs and were perfectly fine before their unwelcome and unsolicited liaison with non-human beings. Until then they could cope with the ups and downs of daily routine because no matter how bad life becomes those things are *normal*. Being taken by space-age dwarves is decidedly *ab*normal.

Most close encounter and abduction victims are not after media publicity or the money on offer from tabloid newspapers for their stories. Many of them would be relieved to discover that their experience was the result of temporal lobe epilepsy or some similar brain malfunction. One abductee, with tears streaming down her face, begged me and the clinical psychologist present to tell her it was just a dream. We could not oblige. Whitley Strieber was convinced at one point that he was going mad and contemplated suicide. The case of Private First Class Gerry Irwin is a prime example of how the phenomenon can screw up someone's life.

Crash Victim

Irwin, a Nike missile technician, was driving back to his barracks at Fort Bliss, El Paso, Texas when he was confronted by the phenomenon. It was late on February 28, 1959, as he headed from Nampa, Idaho and turned south-east on Route 14 when he saw a glowing object cross the sky. Irwin stopped the car and climbed out as the object flew behind a ridge and was hidden from view.

He wondered if he had witnessed an airliner attempting a crash landing and decided to see if he could help. Using boot polish, Irwin wrote 'STOP' on the side of his car and left a note attached to the steering wheel. Half an hour later a fish and game inspector found the note and took it to Cedar City Sheriff Otto Pfief, who organised a search. Ninety minutes after he had set off, Irwin was found unconscious and taken to hospital. There was no evidence of an aeroplane crash.

A Dr Broadbent found that the young man's temperature and respiration were normal. It was as if he was merely asleep, except he could not be woken. Broadbent diagnosed hysteria. When Irwin woke up on March 2 he could not remember what had happened to him. During the twenty-three hours of unconsciousness he spoke in his sleep and mumbled incoherently about a 'jacket on the bush'. When he finally sat up in bed, he asked, 'Were there any survivors?'

Irwin was assured he was not wearing a jacket when found, and was then flown to Fort Bliss to be placed under medical observation at the William Beaumont Hospital for four days. Afterwards, he was returned to duty, although his security clearance was revoked. Several days later, he fainted while walking in the camp, but rapidly recovered. It happened again a few days later in El Paso, so Irwin was taken to hospital. He woke up in the early hours of the next day and asked, 'Were there any survivors?' Irwin was informed the date was March 16, not February 28.

Once again, he was transferred to the base hospital, and placed under observation by psychiatrists for a month. According to a Captain Valentine the test results showed that the private was 'normal'. Discharged on April 17, Irwin seemed to be in the grip of powers he could not control. The following day he gave into a very powerful urge and left the fort without leave, catching a bus in El Paso. He arrived in Cedar City on Sunday, April 19, and walked to the spot where he saw the UFO, then left the road. *Irwin went straight to a bush where his jacket lay.*

There was a pencil in one of the button holes with a piece of paper wound tightly around it. He removed the paper and set fire to it, after which he came out of the trance, but none the wiser why he had visited there. Confused, Irwin turned himself in to Sheriff Otto Pfief, who explained to him the bizarre circumstances surrounding his disappearance seven weeks earlier.

Once more Private Irwin was returned to Fort Bliss, where he underwent a new battery of psychological tests. Again, he was given a clean bill of health. At this point, respected ufologist James Lorenzen contacted Irwin and investigated his story. The case came to the attention of the Inspector General, who ordered a full official investigation, but events were about to take an even stranger turn. On August 1, Private First Class Gerry Irwin failed to report for duty, and a month later was listed as a deserter. It was as if he had disappeared off the face of the Earth. Irwin was never seen again.

It is obvious to anyone who has studied the great wealth of literature on the close encounter experience that Gerry Irwin was suffering post-traumatic stress disorder. Dr Broadbent came nearest when he diagnosed 'hysteria'. But having no knowledge of the UFO phenomenon, the specialists could not find a reason for hysteria. If Irwin had told the psychiatrists he was attacked and robbed they would have known how to treat him. Because there was no *obvious* reason for his strange condition the mental health experts were perplexed.

Gerry Irwin was suffering from amnesia. The key to his condition lay in unlocking the memories buried deep in his subconscious mind. *Who knows what horrors lay buried there?* When Irwin went in search of the 'crashed airliner' he had encountered something too awful for his conscious mind to cope with. The trance-like state that kept overtaking him was perhaps his way of coping with the experience, by trying to switch off from the outside world. Or was there another explanation?

Did the entities have control of Irwin's mind? When, like an automaton, he returned to Cedar City, did a further encounter take place of which he had no conscious memory? What was on the paper which he destroyed? Was it notes or drawings he made before his discovery, or did the paper contain a message from *them*? Irwin came out of the trance when he burned the paper. It reminds us of people put under a magical spell in olden times who could only be released when the words were written down and burned during a ritual.

What happened to Gerry Irwin? When he disappeared that summer was he obeying yet another powerful urge to revisit the scene of the crime? *Was he taken away never to return?*

A Matter Of Record

This case also involves a man's disappearance and an aircraft, but there the similarity ends – except that the perpetrators of the crime were also, apparently, the intelligences behind the UFO phenomenon. The fascinating aspect here is that the pilot gave a radio commentary as the tragic event unfolded, which fortunately was tape recorded.

Frederick Valentich was a twenty-year-old Australian who loved flying. He had recently spent two weeks training at the Melbourne Royal Australian Air Force Base, and was eager for some additional night flying experience. He arranged a flight to King Island on Saturday, October 21, 1978. His father, Guido, attested to the young man's excitement at the prospect. Valentich took $200 with him to bring back some crayfish for his friends.

The weather conditions that evening were perfect for flying. Earlier in the day, Valentich had attended a three-hour course on meteorology. The young man was determined to become a commercial pilot. He climbed into the Cessna 182 rented from Southern Air Services and began his take-off at 6.19 pm. It would not take much more than an hour to complete the flight to Moorabbin Field.

That evening at Tullamarine Airport the acting duty air traffic controller was Steve Roby, a commercial pilot with ten years' experience. He wished Valentich 'a good flight', and reminded him to call when he reached Cape Otway, the point where the Cessna would leave the Victoria mainland and cross the Bass Strait. They talked at Otway: everything was routine. A few minutes later, Valentich radioed to announce he had begun his slow descent to King Island. He was at 1,372 metres, well below radar coverage from Melbourne. Not long afterwards he called Robey, and in a calm voice asked, 'Is there any known traffic below five thousand [feet]?'

The acting duty air traffic controller checked his log and reported that nothing should be there. Valentich explained, 'I … em … seems to be a large aircraft below five thousand.' Robey put in a request for a radar sweep of the area, and then asked the pilot what kind of aircraft it was. He replied: 'I cannot affirm … it has four bright, seems to me like landing lights. The aircraft has just passed over me … about a thousand feet above. Ah, Melbourne, it's approaching me now from due east … towards me. It seems to me that he's playing some sort of a game. He's flying over me two … three times at speeds I could not identify.'

Robey asked the pilot his height in an attempt to keep him calm. Ten seconds later, Valentich returned with the first hint of strain in his voice, saying: 'Melbourne … it's not an aircraft … It is … Ah, it's flying past me. It's a long shape. I, ah, cannot identify more than that … such speed. It's before me right now, Melbourne.'

The air traffic controller asked for more details, then Valentich gave him some startling information: 'Melbourne … it seems like it's, ah, stationary … What I'm doing right now is orbiting and the thing is just orbiting on top of me also. It's got a green light and a sort of metallic like … it's all shiny on the outside.'

At this point, Steve Roby was becoming very concerned. There should not have been anything else out there with the Cessna. Just then Valentich radioed that the object had disappeared and asked Roby whether it was a military aircraft. The cat-and-mouse game had gone on for six minutes, but now Valentich reported a new problem – 'The engine is rough idling … the thing is coughing …' Roby asked him what he was going to do. Now the young pilot sounded afraid. 'My intentions are, ah, to go to King Island. Ah, Melbourne … that strange aircraft is hovering on top of me again. It *is* hovering and it's *not* an aircraft.' Six seconds later he pressed the microphone switch for the very last time. In his panic, Valentich got the call sign mixed up, and that was it. What followed were weird metallic scraping noises, then silence.

An extensive search was launched involving civilian and military ships and aircraft, but no trace of either the pilot or the Cessna 182 were ever found. Valentich's disappearance happened during a time of great UFO activity in the area. One sighting in particular occurred at 2 pm on the same day of the Cessna's final flight, at Currie *over King Island*. Witnesses described how their attention was drawn to a single strange cloud in an otherwise clear blue sky. From this emerged a golf ball-shaped object which flew out to sea, and then returned to disappear inside the cloud. Some photographs were also later produced. They apparently show a strange object in the sky over Cape Otway during the time of the ill-fated flight.

A number of theories were put forward to explain the disappearance. Frederich Valentich made no secret of the fact that he took a close interest in UFOs. Indeed, he kept a scrap-book of newspaper cuttings. Some conjectured it was a joke that got out of hand and resulted with the pilot becoming disorientated and crashing into the sea. That was ridiculous: Valentich would not have risked his future career as a pilot by playing a stupid prank.

It was also suggested that Valentich had used the UFO scenario to fake his disappearance. There was enough fuel in the Cessna to fly past King Island to Tasmania. A similar theory had Valentich planning his suicide and dreaming up the UFO encounter to ensure he made headlines. But the pilot did not apparently have any reason to disappear, never mind kill himself.

The Department of Aviation conducted a lengthy investigation into the case, which was published in May 1982. It concluded, 'The reason for the disappearance of the aircraft has not been determined.' The only explanation that does fit the facts is that Frederick Valentich fell victim to UFO intelligences. Where is he *now?*

Deadly Injuries

Does the UFO phenomenon purposely set out to harm human beings? There is no doubt in my mind that some encounters can result in personal injury and even death, but whether this is deliberate or an accidental by-product of alien activities is open to argument.

I am convinced that the intelligences *have absolute control* over all they do. *Everything is contrived, down to the last detail.* 'Chance' encounters are carefully staged whilst 'crashed' UFOs are nothing more than stage props. Perhaps 'accidental' injuries and fatalities are created on purpose. Why? To reinforce a belief in visiting extraterrestrials, who, like human beings, would be fallible. The injuries provide some proof of UFO reality.

Grilled At Falcon Lake

Stephen Michalak received his 'proof' on May 20, 1967, at Falcon Lake, some eighty miles east of Winnipeg, Canada, where he lived. Something of an amateur geologist, Michalak, a fifty-two-year-old industrial mechanic, was out prospecting.

Having just eaten lunch, his attention was drawn by the cackling of geese. Michalak saw two scarlet lights in the clear sky. Descending, they resolved into cigar-shaped objects with a humped protrusion set in the centre top. One of the objects completed its descent to the ground while its companion hovered over the tree tops for a moment before suddenly accelerating and disappearing into the sky.

Michalak watched about forty metres away behind some rocks as the landed object made a whistling and whining noise. It began to change colour from brilliant scarlet to grey-red, then grey and finally silver. 'Exactly the same effect as hot metal when it cools down,' he said later. Now able to discern more details, he saw it was disc-shaped, about ten-and-a-half metres in diameter with sloping sides and a dome structure above the 'upper deck'. The mechanic counted nine vent-like ducts in a ring around the side. These were about fifteen centimetres by twenty-three.

The craft just sat there. Michalak began to feel more confident. Making several close approaches, he produced some sketches. Michalak was able to see that each of the ducts contained thirty small holes, reminding him of ventilation or exhaust holes. He felt waves of heat coming off the object accompanied by a vile, sulphurous odour, which made him feel nauseous. The smell of sulphur is associated with supernatural evil.

Michalak approached again and saw a doorway appear, from which shone a brilliant violet light that lit up the ground despite the

91

bright sunlight. Although he could not see anyone, the Canadian heard the sound of three voices and attempted to communicate in several different languages, but was unsuccessful. He drew nearer and looked inside. There he noticed a number of small lights flashing in a random fashion throughout the interior. As he stepped back, the doorway closed.

Astonishment and curiosity overcoming his fear, Michalak placed a gloved hand on the shiny surface of the craft. The glove immediately began to melt. He withdrew it. At that moment, the object tilted upwards and Michalak felt a burning sensation on his chest. His shirt burst into flames so he tore it off along with his vest. Then he was sent reeling when a blast of hot air hit him from one of the vents. He glanced up to see that the object was now above the trees – and rapidly disappearing from sight.

Stephen Michalak was now in a distressed state. He collected up his prospecting gear and began the three-kilometre trek back to the Trans Canada Highway. The relatively short distance took him two hours as he felt extremely ill, vomiting many times along the way. On the highway he attempted to flag down a police patrol car, but strangely it refused to stop. When he tried to get some medical assistance no one wanted to know, so the sick man had no choice but to drive all the way back to Winnipeg, where he was immediately admitted to hospital.

For the next eighteen months Michalak suffered from a mysterious malady. Primarily, he was treated for first degree burns, but after his release from hospital a rash appeared on his chest and weight began dropping off him. Every three or four months the symptoms returned. In August 1968, a geometric pattern of burns appeared on his chest, coupled with a feeling of nausea and blackouts. Michalak spent thousands of dollars on doctors bills trying to find out what was wrong. None of the twenty-seven medical specialists who saw him could diagnose his illness.

In view of the reality of Michalak's injuries, an official investigation was mounted involving the Department of Health and Welfare and National Defence, the National Research Council and the University of Colorado. It will come as no surprise to learn that the authorities did not like what they found, and attempted to twist the evidence and throw a veil of secrecy over the affair.

Higher than normal background radiation was recorded at the site, but this was explained as resulting from the luminous dial on the victim's watch! Pieces of metal which were almost pure silver were discovered, too. These had apparently been subjected to intense heat. But most of the report was never made public. When Member of Parliament Ed Schreyer asked the National Department of Defence to release the full report, his request was refused. The results of the laboratory analysis on Michalak's damaged clothes remains an official secret.

Of course, there were those who suggested the whole incident was a hoax, although there was no evidence for this. One ufologist postulated that Michalak had created the burn pattern by heating up a barbecue, then placing the red hot grill against his chest. That would have meant the mechanic was psychologically disturbed, and there would have been other indications of this. Surely it is time that so-called intelligent people used a little bit of common sense when evaluating cases like this? Stephen Michalak was burned by a UFO to provide a little – but not too much – evidence of the reality of aliens. Like Frederick Valentich, he was not the first sacrificial lamb … and would not be the last.

Mark Of The Aliens

As we have seen, the phenomenon can leave its mark on human beings, usually to the detriment of the victim, but sometimes there are benefits. A case in point is that of 'Dr X', a medical doctor from southern France.

On the night of November 1, 1968, he was awoken shortly before 4 am by his fourteen-month-old child. Dr X was in some pain when he climbed out of bed due to an injury to his leg incurred while chopping wood three days earlier. He found the baby gesturing excitedly towards the window. Through the shutters the doctor saw flashes of light, which he assumed were lightening as it was raining heavily. Curiously, there was no peal of thunder. The doctor gave his son a drink of water and inspected the house. The light seemed to be emanating from the same point across the valley, so he walked out onto the terrace for a better look and saw two objects.

They were disc-shaped, silvery white on top and bright red underneath. A cylinder of light projected from beneath each object whilst flashes of light shot across the gap between the UFOs at intervals of about one second. Dr X realised the objects were coming closer, then the two discs merged into one. This new single object flipped over from the horizontal to the vertical position. A shaft of light began sweeping round, flashing across the house and hitting the doctor full in the face. At that moment came a bang and the disc flew away, leaving behind a whitish misty glow which was dispersed by the wind.

Dr X woke his wife and told her of the incident. At this point, she noticed with amazement that the swelling on his leg had completely disappeared, and the doctor realised he was no longer in pain. Dr X immediately sat down, wrote a detailed account and made some sketches. Six days later he was visited by science writer Aime Michel, who took a serious interest in UFOs. Michel found that Dr X was very distressed and had lost weight. There were also pains in his abdomen. A red triangular pigmentation had appeared around his navel.

On the night of November 1, the doctor had a dream in which the triangular pattern was connected with the UFO. Aime Michel suggested that the mark was psychosomatic, but then the same pattern appeared on the child's stomach! By November 17, the triangular phenomenon was well developed. Dr X sought the advice of a dermatologist, without mentioning the UFO sighting. The dermatologist found no cause for the pigmentation, and was so mystified he prepared a paper for the French Academy of Medicine.

Michel kept the witness under close observation for two years and then produced a report on the case. The investigator noted that the doctor's leg remained completely healed, but the strange triangle continued to come and go on both father and son, staying for several days at a time. This would occur on the child even if he was away from home with his grandmother. The triangle has continued to appear every year.

The Legacy Of Ahar

Serious inexplicable illnesses seem to dog victims of alien activity. Briton Dr 'Simon Taylor', a university lecturer in Middle Eastern studies, had a dramatic abduction experience in Iran in September 1976. He was teaching English at the time and formed a close friendship with a distinguished civil servant named Reza. Dr Taylor allowed me access to his extensive notes on the case.

The friends decided to spend the weekend walking in the Elburz Mountains above Tehran. They parked in the village of Ahar and set off in the early evening. The mountain is dotted with cabins so that walkers can escape from the cold nights. After about an hour, Simon and Reza decided to stop for the evening and shared a cabin with a man and his son. They had a light meal, lit a paraffin lamp and eventually bedded down for the night.

Simon awoke some time later gasping for air. He found Reza meddling with the lamp, thinking it was at fault. The man and his son had disappeared, together with their belongings. They became aware of sounds outside the cabin like the snapping of branches or the crackling of burning wood. Suddenly, the cabin was rocked by a series of heavy thumps on the roof. Thinking there was an earthquake the men ran outside, still in their underwear.

Three 'men' with large, lustrous eyes and completely covered in black stood facing them. They reminded Simon of SAS combatants. The friends were told to dress and bring their belongings. This they did, and were then ordered by the entities to follow them down the mountain path. One moment they were walking on the ground – and the next they were inside an oval-shaped room. They were apparently in some sort of craft. The object then took off.

Simon and Reza were able to view the ground through a large window or screen that took up the whole of one wall. After their aerial flight, they were asked to leave, but as soon as they stepped outside the room they found themselves back on the mountain. But now it was midday ... and the pair were just a couple of hundred metres from where they had left the car in Ahar.

The experience had a devastating effect which affected their personal relationship and, more seriously, their physical health. On the way back to Tehran, both men were violently sick, their nerves shattered. This was made even worse because the social stigma attached to the subject meant they could not tell their friends and relatives of the incident. Simon returned to England in December, where he married his fiancée, an Iranian.

Long term physical conditions followed in the wake of the abduction, including crushing headaches whenever the Englishman dwelt on the experience. Around 1977, he developed gynaeco-mastia, an embarrassing swelling of the breasts, and in 1981 was forced to undergo plastic surgery. Further medical complications were to follow. In July 1986, Simon suffered what he thought was a heart attack. In fact, it was pericarditis, an inflammation of the sac around the heart. A year of malaise and fatigue overtook him in 1990, which was eventually diagnosed as post-viral syndrome, myalgic encephalomyelitis, or ME.

Simon told me: 'At first, it felt as though I had a severe bout of 'flu which got worse. The 'flu-like symptoms eased off, to be replaced by excruciating muscle pains and overwhelming fatigue, plus loss of short-term memory, inability to concentrate, aversion to bright lights and loud sounds, unpredictable mood swings and great black stretches of depression.'

To this day, Dr Simon Taylor spends time in and out of hospital being treated for a variety of illnesses. Reading the full transcript of his time aboard the UFO, it seems obvious that events happened to him – and Reza – which neither man could consciously remember. This was hinted at in his statement to me: 'My health problems may turn out to be another legacy of Ahar. I cannot directly attribute them to our experience there, but I do vaguely recollect being touched around the chest region by one of the entities.'

The Cancer Connection

Simon found that Reza would not talk about the experience, except to say that he knew when, where and how he would die. Several other abductees have told me they expect to die before they reach forty. Simon's letters remained unanswered and they drifted apart. From 1979 until 1986, he heard nothing from the Iranian, except for greeting cards marking the Islamic New Year. Then he received a cryptic telephone message from an unknown source. A voice said, '*Reza has joined Reza.*' That persuaded him to call his friend's office number. Simon was told that Reza had died a year ago – almost to the day – of cancer of the liver.

He immediately wrote to Reza's brother and received a letter which detailed the bizarre circumstances of the young man's demise. Apparently, a few days before his death he discharged himself from hospital and travelled hundreds of miles to Mashhad, a town in eastern Iran on the Russian border. There he booked into a guest house. On the evening before his body was found, Reza was spotted near a shrine freely distributing bank notes from a large black bag. The shrine was to the Imam Reza, a descendant of the prophets. *Reza had indeed joined Reza*. His body was found the following morning in his room by a maid. Of Reza's death, Simon told me: 'There was nothing to suggest suicide: no note, no pill bottles, no rope and no gun. Since an autopsy was not performed – it is forbidden in Islamic law – the truth remains a matter of conjecture.'

A number of years ago I investigated a close encounter case that similarly resulted in fatal consequences.

The Bringer Of Death

Ken Edwards was an engineer who drove a company van. After work on the evening of March 17, 1978, he washed and changed, then drove to a trade union meeting in Sale, Cheshire. He departed about 11 pm and began the journey home to Risley near Warrington, on the M62. At what is now Junction 11, Ken left the motorway by an unsigned service road to take a short cut. It was now approaching 11.30. He was less than two-and-a-half kilometres from the end of his journey as he drove along Daten Avenue, which passed through scrubland owned by the Ministry of Defence.

As Ken continued, he approached an embankment on his right and a tall chain-link security fence on his left, which surrounded land belonging to Atomic Energy Authority (AEA). Suddenly, less than a hundred metres ahead, his headlights picked out a strange looking figure at the top of the embankment. Ken began to slow down, eventually stopping at the side of the road.

The being was well over two metres tall with a broad body, wearing a silver coverall. Its head was round like a gold fish bowl, the only features being two round eyes. Most alarmingly, its arms seemed to grow from the *top* of its shoulders. Ken watched with growing horror as the entity stretched out its arms and began walking down the steep incline *at right angles to the ground*. By all the laws of gravity, it should have fallen flat on its face.

After pausing on the grass verge beside the road, it began to cross. Ken sat terrified, gripping the steering wheel, when the being stopped suddenly, and its head swivelled to face him. From the eyes

97

came two pencil slim beams of light which entered the cab for, as it seemed at the time, about a minute. The head turned slowly to face forwards again and the being continued its stiff gait across the road until it was blocked by the fence. It lifted up its arms once more, lowered them – *then walked right through the chain links as if they were not there*!

The entity shambled up the incline on the far side of the fence and disappeared into darkness. Badly shaken, Ken managed to get the van into gear and drive home. He walked in and found his wife Barbara waiting for him, looking worried. It was now 12.30 am. *As far as Ken was aware, the experience had only lasted a few minutes*, but almost forty-five minutes were unaccounted for. He briefly told her what had happened. Barbara then took him to the local police station. The officers were convinced by his story and, together with around twenty-five security guards from the AEA, searched the area, but without success.

However, there was clear evidence that *something* had occurred that night. The radio transceiver fitted in the van would not function when Ken went to work on the Monday. When it was examined, technicians discovered that all the major components had been burned out. They speculated that a power surge travelled down the aerial into the machine, causing the damage. It was cheaper to install a new unit than to carry out repairs.

As for Ken, he discovered that his watch had stopped at exactly 11.45 pm, the time of the encounter. This lent credence to the possibility of a missing time episode and possible abduction experience. When I interviewed Ken that weekend he was both bemused and excited at the same time. He showed me some marks on the fingers of his hand, resembling strong sun burn. This hand had been gripping the steering wheel when the beams of light pierced the windscreen. The more serious consequences of the alien encounter were to emerge much later.

Ken began to complain of pains in his abdomen and went for a check-up. It was discovered that the relatively young man was riddled with cancer. He was just forty-two when he died, three years after his experience with the alien entity. Of course, there is no proof of a direct correlation between the encounter and his fatal illness, but I agreed with Barbara when she told me, 'A thing that can burn skin, stop watches and destroy an expensive radio might well be capable of bringing harm to a human being.'

What happened during the missing time? Did the aliens do something to Ken, as they apparently did to Dr Simon Taylor and his friend Reza? Or was Ken's death a consequence of being exposed to the radiating source of energy from the being's 'eyes'? If so, was there an intent to kill?

Another case where a motorist similarly received burns was investigated by ufologist Tony Green. On March 13, 1980, 'Nick', a sub-contractor, was driving north along the A422 towards Stratford-upon-Avon. Just before 8 pm, he became aware of a cigar-shaped object crossing his line of vision. Completely silent, it was so large that at one point it filled the length of his windscreen. As it passed from view, Nick noticed that the steering wheel was so unbearably hot he had to remove his hands. Even so, his left hand suffered a nasty burn, which needed treatment. Whether Nick experienced any other, more serious, long term illnesses, is not known.

A well documented example of the cancer-generating energies associated with alien activity is the Cash/Landrum affair.

Cash For Cancer

Betty Cash was a Texan restaurant owner who decided to check out a new competitor on the night of December 9, 1980. She was accompanied by her friend and senior staff member Vickie Landrum, who brought along her seven-year-old grandson, Colby. It was around 9 pm when they drove back through a pine forest towards Dayton. Suddenly, they noticed a fiery object in the sky, which quickly dropped to tree top height, hovering over the road about forty metres ahead. Betty brought the car to a halt on the otherwise deserted road.

She described the object as a very bright light with no distinct shape, but her friend discerned a rounded top and pointed bottom, like the configuration of an open parachute. Colby said it was diamond shaped. The witnesses climbed out of the car for a better look. There was a background roaring and bleeping sound throughout the encounter. Occasionally, bursts of flame would jet down from beneath the object, making a noise like a flame-thrower.

Colby became distressed, so he and his grandmother went back inside the car. Betty stayed outside a little longer, but when she took hold of the door handle it was so hot it burned her wedding ring into her finger. The object began to move off. Suddenly, twenty-three Chinook helicopters appeared. They followed the UFO, but kept their distance. Betty arrived home at 9.50 pm after dropping off the others.

Within a short time, symptoms of radiation exposure manifested in the three witnesses. Colby had 'sun burn' on his face and eye inflammation. Vickie Landrum also had inflamed eyes, plus some odd indentations across her finger nails – and her hair was falling out. Understandably, Betty Cash, who had been exposed the longest, suffered the most.

She complained of blinding headaches, nausea, vomiting and diarrhoea. There were also neck pains, swollen eyes and blisters on her scalp which burst, releasing a clear liquid. Betty was admitted to Parkway General Hospital in Houston as a burn victim. Medical specialists were unable to diagnose her symptoms. In just two months her medical bills came to $10,000. Her hair began falling out in clumps. But worst of all, Betty developed breast cancer and had to have a mastectomy. Photographs of the injuries are shocking.

The object resembled nothing the three had ever seen before. Learning the government's official view on UFOs was that they did not exist, the women decided the object must belong to the US military and sued for $20 million. What followed were several years of cover-up and subterfuge by the establishment.

Despite independent witnesses to the Chinooks, the military denied having any knowledge of them! In court were representatives of NASA, the Air Force, Army and Navy. In August 1986, the judge dismissed the case on the grounds that no such device was owned, operated or listed by any branch of the American government. Judge Ross Sterling only heard expert testimony from the various government agencies. Betty Cash, and Vickie and Colby Landrum were not allowed to give any evidence in court.

The case drew a lot of attention in the USA. Not surprisingly, the British media reported none of it. They do not want you to *believe*.

Silence Of The Lambs

Just as alarming is the mutilation of animals by the UFO intelligences. Animals are abducted, too, but most are not returned. Some are, but these are often found with organs surgically removed and drained of blood. One Yorkshire farmer recently told researcher David Cayton how a pet lamb vanished overnight from a secure padlocked shed.

In Northern Ireland, forty-four ewes were slaughtered during one week in January 1985 at a farm in Ballmoney. Archie Rogers of the Ulster Farmer's Union said it was a mystery how they died. All of them had puncture marks to the neck.

I looked into a case of animal mutilation in 1988 at a farm in Rhayader, mid-Wales. This occurred over several weeks from August to October. Thirty-five sheep were found dead with puncture marks to the breast. Several of the carcasses had been taken away for a detailed autopsy by the Ministry of Agriculture. Charles Pugh, the farmer's, son told me: 'The animals were found with four to five small teeth marks. One of them was still alive. It took two weeks to die. This had been happening just three hundred metres from us, but no one has seen or heard anything. It's the strangest thing we've ever encountered in forty years of sheep farming.'

A local hunt were invited onto the land by Mr Pugh on four occasions to track down the predator. Each time the hounds picked up a scent which led to a brook. Charles Pugh told me that he and his father speculated that the culprit might be an otter with a broken tooth, although none had been seen. Government pathologists apparently ruled out dogs or foxes. With permission of the family, I wrote to the Ministry of Agriculture for more information. The department did not even reply.

Similar cases have been reported in Britain and Ireland for decades. During May 1810, seven to eight sheep a night were being silently slaughtered in Ennerdale, Cumbria. The only injuries were puncture wounds to the neck through which all the blood had been sucked out. Over four months in 1874 sheep were discovered killed in Ireland. Up to thirty animals a night died. In forty-two instances the deaths were identical: throats were cut and the blood sucked out, the flesh being undamaged.

After advertising in the farming press, David Cayton was contacted by many farmers with similar stories. Cayton managed to collect some carcasses which showed evidence of mutilation and had them expertly examined by a pathologist. One feature is holes like bullet holes, although no pellets have been found. The programme is on-going. So far the results are intriguing. The mutilations exhibited by these animals are not the same as those perpetrated by natural predators like foxes and dogs. It was discovered that the animals were dead *before* the mutilations took place, although no cause of death has been discovered. The animals are missing ears, heads and internal organs.

The modern wave of animal mutilations began in 1967 when a horse called Lady on a ranch in the San Luis Valley, Colorado, was found with its flesh stripped away, internal organs removed and drained of blood. Since then around 15,000 head of cattle have been discovered in the USA and Canada similarly mutilated.

The problem was so widespread that university and government departments became involved. Oklahoma State University said they were unable to produce veterinary students capable of duplicating what the mutilators had done. Some of the cuts could have been carried out with lasers. Predictably, security departments like the Colorado Bureau of Investigation claimed there was no mystery: the animals had died of natural causes and then been mutilated by magpies. But the ranchers and local police officers vehemently disagreed. At one point Satanists were blamed, although no one was ever caught carrying out the mutilations, and there were no arrests. Law enforcement officers were baffled by a lack of foot-prints and tyre marks.

Every indication is that many of the mutilations are carried out elsewhere, and then the carcasses dumped back from where the animal was abducted. Bits of Lady were located in nearby bushes whilst in another case a cow was found caught in the branches of a tree. In cases where the victim is drained of blood, no blood is found on the ground. In many instances, strange lights have been seen over pastures where later mutilated animals were discovered. A farmer in Witney, Oxfordshire, who found two mutilated lambs on his land in 1998 witnessed a UFO six months earlier. This was reported to the police.

In May 1973, Judy Doraty, her daughter Cindy, her mother and sister-in-law were driving home from Houston in Texas when they saw a strange light hovering over pasture land. Judy stopped the car, and after a short while drove off. Afterwards, Judy suffered from headaches and terrible feelings of anxiety. She was hypnotised by Professor Leo Sprinkle, who apparently unblocked a hidden memory. Judy described seeing a calf being lifted up in a beam of light, squirming to escape. Then she, too, was abducted inside the craft and forced to watch as 'two little men' dissected the animal while still alive. They conveyed to her that 'It's for your betterment.'

Meanwhile, a strange incident occurred on the banks of the River Weaver, near Frodsham, Cheshire, in January 1978. Four poachers out after pheasants observed a silver balloon-like object lift up off the surface of the river and land in a meadow. Several figures in silver astronaut-type suits emerged. They converged on a herd of cows, one of which became paralysed. The beings constructed a cage around it. At this point the young men panicked and ran, but experienced a pulling sensation that dragged at their genitals. One of them later developed marks on his leg *which resembled strong sun burn.*

Mutilations have been reported in other countries, too, the island of Puerto Rico boasting some of the weirdest cases. The first documented killings were in early 1975 when a farmer in Moca lost twenty-nine goats over several days. Twelve were dead, seven wounded and ten abducted. The dead and injured goats had been penetrated with a sharp instrument under the thorax and upper haunches. In all cases there were no signs of blood around the wounds. A wave of killings involving all sorts of animals followed. Many were decapitated, missing sexual and internal organs.

In some instances, a strange, hairy creature was reported running away from the scene of the crime. Mutilations continue on Peurto Rico. The locals have given the mysterious killer a name. They call it the *chapucabra*, or 'goat sucker'.

The Proof
Despite the derision of the sceptics, their 'rational' explanations for animal mutilations have not been proven. The evidence, much of it presented by veterinary surgeons, shows that the slaughter is carried out with surgical precision. In view of the vast numbers of killings, if human predators were to blame, over the years a number of culprits would have been caught and prosecuted. As it stands *there have been*

no reports of anyone witnessing humans carrying out a mutilation. But there are sightings of UFOs and strange beings in connection with the slaughter. It is my view that animal mutilations are clear evidence of alien activity.

Answering *why* the beings are involved in such a bizarre and sickening activity is like trying to look into the mind of an earth worm and working out *its* agenda. However, there are theories, apart from ones like the scalpel-wielding magpie. Some ufologists speculate that the aliens are harvesting DNA in order to create biological entities who can then operate in our environment under the control of the UFO intelligences. It reminds us of Strieber's belief that the aliens 'wear bodies like we wear diving suits'. It is outrageous, of course, but then everything connected with this subject is.

Are human beings butchered in this way? Thousands of people completely disappear every year. Some change identities to escape financial or domestic problems, or die in freak accidents, their bodies never being found. Others are murdered and buried under concrete. *But perhaps some of them are abducted by aliens and never brought back.* Like Frederick Valentich or Gerry Irwin.

There is only one known case of human mutilation which seems to reflect the *modus operandi* of the animal mutilators. In 1995, Brazilian ufologist Encarnacion Zapata Garcia and Dr Rubens Goes presented a series of police photographs showing the mutilated remains of a man found near Guarapianga Reservoir on September 28, 1988. The autopsy report said there were no signs the man had struggled or been bound.

The victim's internal organs had been surgically removed, and flesh cut from the jaw and other parts of the body in a skilled manner. Holes found in the head, arms and stomach were unlikely to have been the result of gun shot wounds, the report concluded. Despite this, other ufologists thought that the dead man had fallen victim to rats and vultures – a familiar reaction by those who do not want to believe.

Why do the UFO beings litter the countryside with the mutilated carcasses of animals? If they disposed of the remains properly no one would be the wiser. Possibly it is just arrogance, or perhaps, as I suspect, like the injuries to human beings, *they want us to believe a little bit – but not too much.*

7

Control Freaks

Those who believe in benevolent beings coming here to save the Earth are in for a shock. As I have demonstrated, while some encounters with aliens appear to be relatively harmless, by far the majority result in psychological trauma or even actual physical harm – evidence indeed of the objective reality of the UFO phenomenon.

One abductee informed me that he was told there were three types of aliens interacting with mankind. The first were good, having our spiritual welfare at heart. The second were bad and wanted to bring us harm. But the worst were in the third group. Indifferent, their intentions towards us were neither good nor bad. My contact told me:

> At least you know how you stand with the first two: they're either friends or enemies. But the third group are devoid of emotion and see us as little more than animals to take part in their cruel and bizarre experiments. Their attitude is that they have a job to do. If it creates confusion and pain, that's just tough.

This seems particularly true of abduction victims. The abductee is told 'Do not be afraid,' just before a needle is inserted into the brain. It reminds us of a lab technician stroking a rabbit as he injects it with a serum that will give it cancer. *Not cruel, just indifferent: doing a job*.

Whitley Strieber described how the aliens inserted an object up his rectum: 'It was almost like it was alive. It was a big, grey thing with what looked like a little cage on the end of it, a little round nubbin about the size of the end of your thumb. And they shoved it into me …'

Strieber had a love-hate relationship with the grey insect-like beings that carried out the procedures on him. One entity in particular which he felt was female held a particular fascination: 'In some sense I felt I might love this being – almost as much as I might my own anima. I bore towards her the same feelings of terror and fascination that I might toward someone I saw staring back at me from the depths of my unconscious.'

When he argued with the entity over what they were doing to him, she said 'We do have a right.' Strieber equated this with our own 'God-given right' to do what we will with the lesser species of the Earth. He ponders, 'How odd it was to find oneself suddenly under the very power that one so easily assumes over the animals.'

As we have already seen, that power – which the alien phenomenon exercises over every aspect of our lives, community, environment and culture – seems awesome. However, nothing is more devastating than the loss of personal freedom and the ability to make a choice. More than anything, the phenomenon seeks to control us as individuals. The alien abduction experience is a vivid and terrifying illustration of this.

Over the years I have been involved in the investigation of many abduction cases, assisted by several psychologists. I've taken part in dozens of radio and television debates with professional sceptics, whose attitude often makes my blood boil. *The majority of these people have not investigated a single case*: they just *know* there is nothing more to the phenomenon than misidentifications, brain malfunctions and hoaxing. Debunkers talk about 'temporal lobe epilepsy' and 'sleep paralysis' as causes of 'false memories', even though experiments aimed at proving this have failed miserably.

Worst of all, the sceptics foster the idea that most percipients *want* to have a UFO experience. It is nothing more than their own imagination and internal fantasies creating wish fulfilment. I can say with all honesty that some of the most objective people I have met in connection with this subject are abductees. They do not have a belief system in extraterrestrials or spaceships, and remain objective as regards the source of their experiences. Yet they do know that the experience was real and not fantasy. Contrary to what the sceptics want the public believe, abductees would *love* to learn 'it was just a dream'. The alternative is too terrible for them to contemplate.

The professional sceptics cannot handle it when they are confronted with data which falls outside their scripted responses. In January 1999, I was a guest on a Granada television programme along with a well-known sceptic. During filming I was asked to detail an abduction I had investigated. The case involved a company director and his wife, an executive for a major charity, and their eight-year-old daughter. I described how while travelling through France the couple experienced a missing time episode of around three hours, how they had been followed on the autoroute by a strange aerial object, and how, afterwards, the woman and her daughter discovered they were bleeding. Before the experience, the couple were sceptical about stories of UFO encounters. In the weeks afterwards, the woman reported flashbacks of being inside a cone-shaped object composed of 'a solid blackness'.

The television presenter, Becky Want, then turned to the resident sceptic for his explanation. I was amazed when he ignored my case entirely and rambled on about people waking up from sleep and imagining there are strange figures in the room. When I confronted him with this, first of all he said my case was 'atypical' because it was 'a waking abduction experience'. Then, with a note of desperation, he added, 'Maybe they are making it up.'

The sceptics really should do their homework. Waking abduction experiences *are not* atypical! But even the debunkers' blind scepticism serves a purpose. Sceptics ensure we believe in the phenomenon a little bit, *but not too much*. They sow doubt and confusion and allow the beings to go about their business in total freedom.

One to One

More than any other aspect of close encounter experiences, abductions illustrate the devastating emotional effects of one-to-one alien activity. 'Mary Everett' contacted me in 1989 to relate a UFO sighting and a few scraps of 'memory' which puzzled her. I went and carried out an interview to elicit as much information as possible from her conscious mind.

Mary, a nursing auxiliary, described how she was sitting in the front room of her terraced house when she saw three lights through the window. She went and opened the front door for a better view. In the sky at a low elevation were three lights in a triangular configuration – white on top, red bottom left and green to the right. At first, Mary wondered if it was an aircraft, but the lights seemed to be stationary. Suddenly, they went out. In their place appeared a structured object hovering over waste ground where houses had been demolished. It was dome-shaped with a nipple on top and a strip of square lights around the skirt, which flashed like the flash on a camera. After a few minutes the object vanished in mid-air.

During the sighting Mary heard no sound. In fact, there was no noise at all, despite the fact she lives near a main road. There was something else wrong, too. The sighting lasted just a few minutes, but when she came back indoors around three-quarters on an hour had passed. Though it was winter, Mary did not feel cold, considering the *apparent* time she spent on the doorstep.

Since then several impressions have plagued her. One was a sensation of floating, another was of someone placing a small square of material on her forehead, and the third was of 'a sharp cut in my private parts'. Mary also had the impression that while in bed one wall of the room disappeared and she was transported through it. There was also the image of a being with oriental-type features at the side of her bed. These impressions played on Mary's mind over the intervening years. She agreed for me to arrange hypnosis to explore the experiences further.

Hypnosis is not a truth drug. No one can guarantee that what emerges under hypnosis is the objective or partial truth, embellished with fantasy. However, it has been used successfully in clinical therapy where the subject is enabled to confront buried memories of traumatic episodes and in the process exorcise them. Hypnotic regression *can be* a short cut to memory retrieval when someone is suffering from amnesia. However it must be stressed that it is not possible to verify Mary's hypnosis testimony.

I outlined Mary's case to Jim Singleton, a clinical psychologist who worked at a major hospital in the north of England, and he agreed to help. Jim had successfully liaised with me before on the Ilkley Moor abduction case. Three sessions of hypnosis took place in the summer of 1989.

The Price Is Right
At the time of the UFO sighting Mary was reading in her living-room. She switched on the television to watch a particular programme, but the long-running games show *The Price Is Right* was just starting. Realising she had on the wrong channel, Mary was about to change

over when she saw the lights through the window. She stood up and opened the front door.

> I was waiting for a programme to come on. That aeroplane's coming low. Three lights, and they've gone out! And there's a silver thing. I don't know what it is. It's no aeroplane ... It doesn't look all that big. It's silver and round, and I don't know whether the lights are going round or they're taking photographs [flashing] *I can't move*!

Mary finds she is paralysed, which usually marks the beginning of an abduction episode. Paralysis is common in entity encounter experiences. Mary is intrigued by the strange object, so decides to stretch across and alert her neighbour by knocking on the door. It is when she attempts this she discovers she cannot move. Her frustration and fear are evident:

> I'm going to knock on Barbara's door! I'm here and there's a little wall, and all I have to do is stretch across and knock on Barbara's door and she'll see it. But I can't move ... I'm just looking at the silver thing. I wish someone would come onto the street. I'm just there and these lights are going round. It's gone! Didn't go up, didn't go down, didn't go sideways – just gone! Got to go in now. Got to sit down in my chair.

When we asked her how long she had been outside, this was Mary's reply, 'When I came in that stupid programme was just finishing.'

The *The Price Is Right* ran for about fifty minutes. Mary said she then rang up George, a friend, to see if he had seen the object. George said he had not, so Mary made herself a cup of tea and sat down. A feeling stole over her that she had been 'honoured' to see the object. She viewed this invading thought with hostility, without knowing why. Then she told us, 'I saw it in the sky, *but I had a feeling it had come from the Earth.*'

We then asked her to cast her mind back to the time when she thought there was someone in her bedroom and she experienced a cut in her genitals. Without realising it, we were going directly to perhaps what was the most traumatic episode of the experience. Mary slipped back in time and started to re-live the incident. Her recollection began with a deep sigh.

> I'm going to bed. I'm tired. [Yawns and begins to snore, then whispers and sounds afraid.] It's cold. [Whispers unintelligibly and her whole body starts to shake.] It's cold … it's cold … stairs … go away … what's he doing? Little square … little square … shrinking on my forehead. Little square on my forehead. It's shrunk. There's a light. Don't do that!
>
> [At this point, she is shaking violently. Her arms and legs are drawing protectively into a foetal position. Mary's face is strained, and tears form in her eyes. What happens next is unexpected and made even more awful by the twilight conditions of the unlit room. The light is fading outside. In her living-room, Mary lets out a cry and begins to sob. She sounds like someone under torture, or a woman at the mercy of a rapist. It is terrible as she begins to beg, punctuated by bouts of sobbing as she is violated in some unstated way.]
>
> Leave me alone … [Her words are difficult to hear through her sobs. Now the tears are trickling down her cheeks.] Leave me alone … *Leave me alone* … [She becomes hysterical. All the while, Jim and I remain seated in silence at the opposite ends of the room, and I wonder, '*Why doesn't he do something?*']

There was a lull in Mary's narration. Jim asked her, 'Can you tell me what's happening there?' Her sobbing then became more powerful. In the midst of it she cried one last time, 'Leave me alone …' Then the sobbing stopped and there was a deep sigh.

Mary's eyes snapped open, but she remained motionless. Moments earlier, she played out the role of someone who had no hope of escape. But now, in this re-enactment, there *was* escape – spontaneous emergence from the state of hypnosis. Then I understood why Jim had done nothing to alleviate Mary's suffering: she could do it herself. I was stunned by what had just happened. Out of hypnosis, but still visibly upset, we asked Mary why she was in such a state.

I don't know – I wasn't cut there, and I don't [consciously] remember crying and saying "Leave me alone." [Loud sigh and pause.] When I first told Peter this story, I sensed there was someone at the side of the bed and they seemed – they seemed to put something on my forehead. But I wasn't frightened, and I was very, very cold. When they … [Sigh] when they put a little square on my forehead it seemed to shrink. Once this had shrunk, I seemed to be calm. When I first told Peter, all I remembered after that was this Chinese coming towards me, with someone behind him, and I got a sharp cut between my legs. I wasn't crying or saying "Leave me alone".

Was the incident she had supposedly just re-lived under hypnosis a different one from the encounter Mary partially remembered? She could not understand why she was so upset when in her conscious recollection the square which was placed on her forehead rendered her calm and relaxed.

Despite the distress it caused her, Mary insisted that Jim should hypnotise her again and send her back. This we did after a cup of tea to calm Mary's nerves. The second session continued from where the first had abruptly ended. Evidently, she was still under the control of the beings and undergoing some sort of invasive examination. Jim asked her what was happening. Mary replied with several sighs and a long pause. When she did eventually speak, it was with a rush of angry words aimed at her captors.

You can take that bloody light away! Go on! [Deep sigh] They're trying to read my mind, but they're not going to. [Then in a loud voice] *Sing a song of sixpence, a pocket full of rye* … That'll fool them, won't it? Take that light away. [Loud again] *Sing a song of sixpence* … Just keep quiet … Why won't they take that light away? I'm not going to look at that light. Take that bloody light away! [She makes murmuring noises now, obviously very afraid. For the last few minutes, her right hand has been slipping off the settee and back onto the coffee table, where she immediately snatches it back. Mary is whispering unintelligibly as if these are her private thoughts.] Go away ... light ... oh ... oh ... they keep lifting my hand up. Putting my hand over there ... [Sighs] Oh ...

Jim asks her what is happening. Mary starts whimpering quietly like a trapped animal.

Can't move my ... can't move my ... [Whimpers loudly, obviously in some distress.] Don't ... don't go under there. Control Mary ... *Sing a song of six* ... [Cries] Don't want to put my hand over that light. [Whimpers. The words which follow are broken up as she has great difficulty getting them out.] Bl ... blue ... blue ... li ... light ... blue light ... coming towards me. [Whimpers. Sighs.] Putting things here ...

Under questioning, Mary described how 'they' were putting an apparatus on her head. Once again she started reciting the nursery rhyme in an attempt to stop the beings listening to her thoughts. The scene suddenly shifted.

I'm in another room now. Lying on a table. It doesn't have any wheels, only a centre piece. [Sounds afraid] Lying on my own; there's nobody else in the room. I'm fr ... fr ... frightened. *S ... S ... Sing a song of sixpence* ... There's no ... no light. There's no big light. [Her voice is shaky as if she is trembling with cold or fear.] This time, I'm just lying on the table, lying on the t ... t ... table. [Starts shivering] T ... T ... Two people come in.

A long pause follows. We ask her what is happening. 'I'm just being left alone. I'm just laying here in this dome-shaped thing and I haven't got that thing on my forehead.'

There is another long pause, then Mary described some kind of symbol or motif on the wall. It was comprised of three short parallel lines in a horizontal configuration, with an angled, almost vertical, line at each end. She likened the symbol to the identification numbers on the side of aircraft. Then Mary started shivering again and became distressed. Once more the middle-aged woman spontaneously emerged from hypnosis. Again, she was disturbed by the strange images that she 'remembered', and their ramifications.

Mary's conscious recollection that these events happened in her bedroom now appeared false, or at best incomplete. She had been taken inside a domed room at some point. Was this some kind of recovery room? As a subsequent hypnosis session showed, we seemed to be dealing with at least three separate abduction incidents. In one, she went to bed and then remembered seeing a wall of her bedroom disappear. That reminds us of the Iranian case where the two men stepped into the UFO from the mountain path, as if they were passing from one dimension of reality into another. Is this what happened to Mary?

Is that what the aliens are capable of? Can they penetrate our reality at any point in space, whether it is in the atmosphere, inside a building or even underground?

We questioned her about the entities that were in the room. She said there were two, about 163 centimetres tall, dressed in silver one-piece suits. Mary could not remember their faces or hands. Although there was no breast outline, Mary *knew* they were female. They kept putting her hand on the 'white thing' and kept wanting her to take a drink. During the whole time neither of them spoke to her.

Mary also said that initially her abdomen was covered by a blanket, but then it disappeared. She added it was a rusty brown colour with gold criss crosses all over it. Somehow, it had a calming effect on her. Despite the extra detail, we still seemed to be dealing with fragments from several different episodes. I wondered about the time scale of the entire episode. We still had not breached the memory of the 'Chinaman' and the 'cut' to Mary's genitals, or was this too painful for the woman ever consciously to recollect?

Mary never lost her objectivity. After the second session of hypnosis, she commented: 'If anyone had mentioned to me, years ago, any of this, I couldn't have believed them. I mean, I went to bed – how can anyone take you from your bed? *How the heck can anyone take you from your bedroom*? In all honesty, if it happened, it's so unbelievable. I can't believe it. Does that sound odd? Things just like that can't happen, can they?'

The Final Session

We did not know it at the time, but the hypnosis session we arranged for September 12 was to be our final attempt at recovering

Mary's lost memories. However, this session revealed a more cohesive story of what happened on the night of the UFO sighting – outrageous though it seemed.

Hypnotic regression can open the door to the subconscious, to a greater or lesser degree. That depends on the monsters imprisoned there, hidden from the conscious mind because they are too terrible to face. Quite often one session of hypnosis makes subsequent forays into the subconscious easier once the door has been opened a crack. In Mary's case it was no different. Jim induced her into the hypnotic state and she began by clearly stating that the incident had occurred one Saturday in October 1985 at a quarter to eight. Once again, she described how the UFO's lights flashed, but this time added something new when we asked her to describe what was happening:

Well, that beam's come down. That beam – the light.

We requested more details about the 'beam'.

The three lights have gone out and there's just this silver thing. [Sigh] And there's nobody on the street. It's very dark. This beam comes down at a diagonal at me, and it's like a fluorescent light with a blue tint at the end. *It's an honour to see it.* This light says it's an honour. Huh! And I'm not frightened, just curious. [Pause, sigh, starts to whimper quietly and her face contorts.] This silver thing's just gone. I'm feeling very cold now, and I'm uneasy, frightened. There's a feeling about it.

She is referring to the beam of light. We ask her to explain more. Mary sniffles and sounds nervous.

When I first saw this light I was at ease, but I'm not at ease now. Because it's very cold, and it doesn't feel nice. And I can't shout out. Calmer now. [Deep breaths, pause, exhales.] There seemed to be an invisible beam as well. I know this sounds silly, but there was an invisible beam which touched my forehead. That was when I got cold and frightened.

Further new images come into Mary's mind as she is back there, standing in the doorway of her house. As she struggles with the fear, her breathing becomes erratic.

It's like two shadows walking through my hedge [Sounds afraid.] They're like two people wearing silver suits with slitted eyes. I'm only four feet eleven and they're smaller than me. I can't move. I can't *move*! [The sobbing returns and her voice begins to stutter and break up.] There's these two silver people coming through the ... the hedge ... One of them has something in his hand. I can't make out what it is, but it's made my hand go very cold and I can't move. Somehow, I know that thing is still there even though I can't see it, and there's an invisible beam coming down from the sky. *Oh God*, I know they've done something – *I'm not on my doorstep any more*!

What Mary is about to relate may refer to a later incident, or the same encounter a little later in the night.

This time it was one silver man on his own, and he came through the wall, not my hedge. [Sniffles and starts to sound upset, sighs and pauses.] The front of my house has a bay window and under it there is a glass cover at an angle covering access into the cellar. This silver man that's walked through my wall has w ... walked ... right through the glass! [Very afraid now and upset.]

I'm not on my doorstep, and I don't know where I am! [Deep breaths, sniffles and sobs.] There's an invisible beam and it's as if you go into this beam and you're not there! You're invisible ... [Mary is now almost hysterical. Her face is contorted, closed up tight.] Will I ever see my home again? [Uncontrollable sobbing now.] Where am I going? [She calms down suddenly.]

I'm on this table now, and I can see my body again. [More sobs and sniffles. Mary feels her body reassuringly.] At least I've got a body again, now ... I don't know who put me on the table. It was as if I was invisible, and then all of a sudden my body reappeared. There was nothing on the table and now my body's there, and I've got a thumping headache. [Sighs, pauses.] There are two people and they're coming towards me. They're putting this thing on my forehead. [Sigh] I think it's a piece of yellow material about three inches by one. He puts it on my forehead and it shrinks. [Sighs] It's shrinking ... I'm feeling a bit more relaxed.

I asked Mary to describe her surroundings.

It's a queer shaped room. I can't see all of it. It's as if I'm in a round corridor. There's a grey, round pillar in the centre, and I'm next to it. More people have appeared now, walking about. I can't see where they come from, I can't see any doors. You look and they're not there, and then two people are there.

During his abduction in Iran, Dr Taylor similarly described how the beings walked into the room from nowhere. Mary asks us to wait a minute while she lifts her head up 'because they have to put a box under it'.

Don't know whether I've got clothes on or not, but I've got this cloth over me. It's like a burnt rusty colour with a gold diamond in it, and it covers me just here. [She indicates from her stomach to the top of her thighs.] Don't know what this box is for, though. They're fetching something like a little machine with wires. It's like a drip. They're putting it here – but it's not a drip. I'm drinking this blue stuff now. Put it down there. [She goes through the motions of picking up a glass, drinks from a glass, then places it back down.]

Oh, I'm very relaxed now. It goes all the way through my body so they can see through it. They're fetching something in now and putting it over my head, like a hair dryer. Somehow this thing is connected to the box under my head. Doesn't hurt, though. I can't feel it. Those wires have to go on my forehead. [She indicates her temples.] Don't know whether it's the box, the "hair dryer" or the wire thing, but I feel very sleepy. They're fetching that light now, and I have to hold my hand over it. That relaxes you and makes you go to sleep.

Mary then told us they wanted to see her fingers. She held out her right hand, extending her fingers one at a time for examination.

They're fetching something now and I have to put my hand on it. I don't know whether they want to take my palm print or what they want. There you are: *for future reference*, you see. They want reference off the other one now, and they want to take scrapings from under my nails. They just got a thing and went like that, and my nails are clean.

Mary now came up with a piece of information which illustrated how clever and cunning the beings were.

When they take a sample of blood from your ear they take it from *behind*. Otherwise if you looked in a mirror you'd see a little red spot, so they take it from behind your ear so you don't know it's been taken.

Suddenly, inspiration floods her face.

I know what's happening with that box now! [She sits upright and feels at the back of her head.] It's to do with these bones. They put fluid in them, you see. That's what that box is for. [She looks momentarily confused.] No – they're taking fluid *out*. [Exhales] That headache again! Think it's got something to do with these sparks going across here.

She indicated her forehead, so we asked her to explain.

It doesn't hurt; it gives you a headache. I'll be glad when they take these wires off my head. Ooh ... you feel really tired when that box is taken away. It's as if they've drawn all

117

your energy from you. Oh, they're taking that off my head now. I feel shattered. I want to hold my hand over the light again. [Pause] Back of my head is aching now from where they took the fluid. [Sighs, grunts and groans as she turns on the couch.] Think I could sleep for a thousand years!

Well, that's all they're going to do for me this time. They're going to come back another time for the rest of the stuff. [Pause. Sighs.] My head feels as if it's on fire! They're taking everything away now. Everybody seems to be vanishing. They're gone! I don't feel frightened now. I'm just floating back now. It's as if I come down on an invisible beam. And they're going to put me back on my doorstep. Well at least I can move now! I'm going in. It's about quarter to nine. [Pauses, then sighs.] Got to rest, then I'm going back again, see? *They'll come back for me in four months.*

We decided at that point it was not in Mary's best interest for us to carry on with further hypnosis sessions. Despite the fact she wanted to know more, there was no denying the obvious stress the encounters generated. She agreed, and we were left to mull over the emotionally-charged contents of the three sessions.

Should we accept Mary's hypnosis testimonies at face value? Are people really taken away for examination and experimentation? Mary remembered a cut to her genitals, although the 'memory' never surfaced under hypnosis. If this had a basis in fact, did it support other cases where aliens apparently extracted sperm and ova to create hybrid beings? Surely Mary was too old for use in breeding experiments?

Mary's account, and the emotional way she reacted under hypnosis, does have a ring of truth about it. But what version of the truth? Her terror was so utterly convincing it made me feel sick to witness it. When she recited the nursery rhyme to 'stop them reading my thoughts', it reminded me of prisoners of war who adopt the same method to blot out the effects of torture.

If we accept that the aliens are interdimensional beings who seek absolute control over us and our environment it makes sense that they would want to manipulate our physiological systems, too.

The apparatus Mary described during her ordeals may have been theatrical props, or the crude psychological interpretations of a technology so 'alien' her mind could not fully grasp it. However, in essence, procedures of some sort did take place. *Was it a coincidence that not long after the UFO sighting she developed abnormal cells in her uterus*? As we have already seen, cancers and other illnesses can follow in the wake of encounters with the Little People. Fortunately, in Mary's case her cancer was successfully treated.

At the commencement of her UFO sighting, Mary described how everything went quiet, and there was no traffic or people in the street. Again, this takes us back to fairy lore where the unwary traveller comes under a spell, or enchantment, cast by the fairies. This enchantment can affect other creatures in the vicinity, too. Stories often describe how even the birds stop singing. I investigated a case where a headmaster and his family observed a brightly lit kite-shaped object which hovered over their house for several minutes. The man commented to me, 'The strange thing was that normally the road outside the house is very busy at that time of the night, but while that thing was there the road was empty.'

I have heard similar comments from dozens of witnesses. Many encounters seemed especially staged for one particular individual or group of people, but in order for that to be effective the absence of other potential witnesses would have to be secured. But what is the mechanism that allows the beings to do that?

The Umbrella Of Perception

A rule of thumb as to whether a UFO sighting is indicative of the real thing or represents mundane phenomena is usually determined by the number and spread of witnesses. The sighting of an object by many people over a wide area is nearly always explained an as astronomical happening, such as fireball meteors. For instance, on New Year's Eve 1978 hundreds of witnesses from Cumbria in north-west England to the north Wales coast reported a brightly lit elongated object. It was, in fact, the booster rocket from Cosmos 1068 – a Soviet satellite – re-entering the atmosphere and burning up.

Conversely, I investigated a case which occurred on Friday August 1, 1980, in the Abram area of Lancashire. This featured the appearance of several objects from late evening to the early hours of

Saturday morning. The main player was a low level, cigar-shaped object which had the capability of hovering and rotating from a horizontal to a vertical position, emitting flames in absolute silence from its rear. At different times during the night it was observed alone, with two attendant spheres of light and with a triangular shaped craft. The electrics in the car of one witness were affected when one of the spheres converged on it down a country lane.

I spoke to over a dozen witnesses who independently of one another described the same phenomenon. Despite a plea in a local newspaper no one else came forward. There is no doubt that this was a genuine phenomenon, *yet why were there not more witnesses*? If this had been an aerial display by the RAF, hundreds of local people would have seen it. Why was this different?

It was because of cases like these that I formulated a theory called the Umbrella of Perception. Alien activity does not occur randomly. Because much of human activity is random this is a hard concept to grasp. The UFO phenomenon is a force of control. It controls and is in control of itself. The concepts of chaos and random behaviour are meaningless in the alien vocabulary. UFO events are staged for certain people. In order to ensure that they – and only they – take part in the show an umbrella of perception is thrown over the general area.

Under the umbrella, the perceptions of everyone are controlled, including percipients and non-percipients alike – the blind and those chosen to see. Mary described how, when she stood on the doorstep watching the object, she could not hear traffic on the nearby main road. This was probably because she was put into a state of altered consciousness by the phenomenon in readiness for her abduction. She also remarked she was surprised there was no one out on the street, and no traffic passing through. Are non-percipients *made* to keep away? Is the phenomenon using mind control?

It could be quite subtle. How many times have you decided to leave the house when a thought intrudes into your head and you wait a while? How many times when out driving have you changed your mind at the last moment and taken a different route? *Can we be sure that these invasive thoughts are always our own?* Surely, though, there should have been some other witnesses to Mary's UFO? It is quite probable there were. But they may have perceived it entirely differently.

In the early hours of February 24, 1979, local businessman Mike Sacks was up seeing to his son, who had tonsillitis. Mike lived with his family in the small village of Stacksteads in the Rossendale Valley near the border with West Yorkshire. As he gave his son a glass of water, the bedroom was suddenly filled with a pulsing light. Mike and his wife watched an orange ball of light head towards a nearby quarry. It stopped abruptly and the light changed to a dim blue, exposing details of a structured craft. The quarry walls were bathed in light as the object, about twice the size of a double decker bus, dropped silently into it.

After fruitlessly waiting for the UFO to reappear, Mike got dressed and drove the four miles to pick up his brother. They visited the quarry and there met two police officers, who also saw the UFO. Mike and his brother left the officers and went down into the quarry. There, a very strange event happened. As they walked along the quarry bottom, Mike was aware of a large structure with a line of brightly lit windows. Before he could react, the words 'Portakabin ... Portakabin' pounded through his head. Convinced there was nothing unusual in the quarry, the two men went home.

Later, Mike thought again about the Portakabin and, as he told me, wondered *what the hell one was doing in the middle of the night with all its lights on*. A few days later he went back to the quarry during daylight and spoke to the foreman. Mike asked him where they had moved the Portakabin because it was not there. The man replied: 'What Portakabin? There's never been a Portakabin.'

Mike walked right past the object as it sat in the quarry, *but something interfered with his perceptions and convinced him it was only a Portakabin*. Perhaps there were witnesses to Mary Everett's UFO, but all they perceived was an aircraft because that is what the phenomenon *wanted* them to see. Inside the Umbrella of Perception, *they* control your thoughts.

Mary's Murky Past

Despite the drawbacks of hypnosis Mary's testimony had a huge emotional impact on me. Her reactions as she 're-lived' the abductions were very convincing. If Mary had been acting, she deserved an Oscar. But Mary had no acting ability and did not want to believe it was true. At one point she begged us to tell her it was just a fantasy, a nightmare that had spilled over into her waking life. In all honesty we could not do that. But something else that emerged during the final session chilled me to the bone.

As Mary described the various procedures the beings apparently carried out on her, I asked if she knew why they were doing it. Her reply was casual yet out of the blue: 'Oh, they've been doing it since I was a baby. They have to keep an eye on me, you see. When I was two they said they were going to look after me.'

Mary, still under hypnosis, then explained how they had come for her every few years: 'When I was seven, when I was four and when I was two they came to visit me. They couldn't take my palm print until I was seven, you see. When you're seven there's different lines on your left hand. You haven't got those lines when you are two and four. Up to seven, they're more interested in looking at the bottom of your feet and behind your ears.'

Mary recollects being in hospital with impetigo, a skin disease:

I don't know whether I was three-and-a-half or four, but it was summer. It was a beautiful summer's day! Beautiful ... and I had a little white gown on. I am the youngest girl there, and I have a bedroom to myself, and I look out into the garden ...

Something happened to Mary in hospital. In order for the doctors to treat her skin disease they had to shave off all her hair. But before doing so, Mary remembers the beings visiting her and cutting off some of her curls.

Mary's child-like trust in the beings is touching – and stomach churning. They wheedled their way into her life like a paedophile seduces and abuses his young victims This love/hate relationship between the victim and the good guy/bad guy role of the abusers is not confined to this case. Not at all. Whitley Strieber and many other abductees have experienced it, too. It brings us back to the lab technician stroking the rabbit before injecting it with an experimental serum which might make it ill, or even kill it. All in the name of science. Just doing a job.

8

Dark Angel

The following case reinforces many of the points I have all ready made. It involves a thirty-two-year-old civil servant called 'Robert Shawe', who initially contacted investigator Alicia Leigh with his UFO sighting.

Alicia, with the assistance of fellow researcher Tony Eccles, interviewed Robert and examined the location. It was obvious that the young man was greatly troubled by something he could not remember, so Alicia asked for my assistance. I helped conduct the subsequent investigation and involved Dr Moyshe Kalman, who carried out hypnotic regression. A psychoanalyst, Dr Kalman has assisted me in many other cases.

The event occurred on the evening of Christmas Day 1994. Moyshe put Robert into a state of hypnosis and took him back in time. During that first session, Alicia and Robert's brother, Daniel, were also in the consulting room with us. Occasionally, the brother put his head in his hands as Robert's frightening and graphic story emerged. In order to appreciate the young man's experiences it is necessary to understand something about his personality and background.

Robert is a shy, introspective individual, who lives alone in a second floor flat on the edge of woodland. His solitary existence is not through choice. Despite relationships with a number of women none of them has worked out. Yet he has plenty of friends and is close to his family. Why, then, did he break with tradition and decide not to spend the evening of Christmas Day with them? On Christmas Eve, Robert found himself in Woolworths looking at decorations for the small artificial tree that stood in the picture window of his flat. The tree was studded with coloured lights, but needed some tinsel to finish off the effect.

That night, he took out a friend, a girl called Susan, to a local pub for a drink. The bar was full of juke box music and revellers enjoying the party mood. Despite this, Susan confided in Robert that she was lonely, having just finished with her boy friend. Later in the evening,

Robert introduced Susan to a young man he knew called Andrew. The couple hit it off immediately. 'I'm kind of glad,' he told us. 'They started talking and looked happy, so I feel I've done something good.'

Robert returned with Andrew to Susan's house, where they continued the Christmas celebrations with her mother. After a few drinks Robert fell asleep on the settee and awoke Christmas morning with a hangover. Following tea and toast, he set off for his mother's house, which was just a five minute walk away. The family were gathering there for Christmas dinner. As they tucked into the turkey, Robert's sister turned to him. 'Carol asked me what I'm doing tonight, and said she'll phone me later to see if I want to come round to her place. I'm not really in the mood for that.'

After dinner, he left for home, telling his mother he might see her later, although he doubted it. In the flat, Robert decided he would go to Manchester city centre that evening after catching up on some sleep. At around four in the afternoon, Robert booked a taxi to pick him up at ten that evening. Then, still fully dressed, he collapsed onto the bed and slept for a few hours.

> It's like I've ordered this taxi. It's as if I don't know where I'm going. There's a destination, but I can't … I'm not heading to a particular place.

After waking, Robert had a bath, shaved and dressed, ready to go out. He put on a dark blue shirt, black trousers and laid out his pig skin jacket on the bed. Carol phoned at one point to see if he was joining the party at her house. He declined the offer, explaining he wanted to be by himself. Carol said afterwards that her brother had not sounded his usual self. In retrospect, it seems that Robert was deliberately alienated from his family in readiness for an encounter experience.

The Fairy Lights
At around a quarter to ten, he put on the television to kill time before his taxi was due. Robert lay across the Chesterfield settee watching a comedy when something caught his attention through the window.

'It's those lights,' Robert explained under hypnosis, 'like a Christmas tree, the lights on a Christmas tree.'

There were about five pinkie-red lights in a vertical zigzag formation as if they were attached to a column of some sort, as

Robert explained to us: 'I'm looking at them through the trees. The leaves have fallen and I can see right through them. The lights are so pretty. At first they were high, then they dropped. They're coming down so slow, so steady, controlled, yet keeping formation. I get the impression they're connected to something, a dark mass.'

As the lights drew level with the trees just yards away from the flat, Robert remarked at how beautiful and intensely bright the lights were. Strangely, they did not illuminate the landscape.

'You'd think they would light the woods up,' he continued, 'but they're not doing that. It can't be a helicopter, because the trees would be moving. It's a strange sight ...'

Both Dr Kalman and I wondered at the similarity between the lights observed through the window and the gaily decorated Christmas tree in the room. Was their a prosaic explanation to all this? In an effort subtly to steer Robert in this direction, Moyshe asked him: 'What do those lights remind you of? They're so beautiful, aren't they?'

Under hypnosis, Robert replied: 'Later on, I was looking at the Christmas tree, trying to gauge the colour of the lights, checking to see it wasn't a reflection in the window.'

'Can you stand between the tree and the window,' Moyshe asked, 'so you would see it was not a reflection?'

Robert was clear in his answer. 'It wasn't a reflection because I could see the tree lights to the left, and I was watching this thing to the right.'

He said later that they were as big as golf balls held at arm's length. The lights came down into the clearing, and Robert decided he had to go outside and investigate. Moyshe reminded him it was almost time for the taxi, but Robert swept it aside, saying: 'That doesn't matter. I've got to see this thing.'

Dr Kalman asked him what was happening next.

I've got my jacket on, gone straight out, downstairs, coming out of the flats. Malcolm Riding is there with his girl friend. They're asking about a party. It's in the end block, but I'm not sure which number. I was going to ask if he'd come over and look with me, but I feel daft because he's with his girl, and let them go. Then I went to the clearing ...

But something happened to Robert in the clearing that is edited from his memory. He recalls: 'I went so far, then thought it was best to turn around. Can't see the lights, but know there's something there. I saw something come down: there's got to be something there! I know I've got to turn back now because that was it, that was the show, that's all I was meant to see.'

Robert returned to the flat and noted it was now half past ten. It seemed only minutes ago he walked outside, but over half an hour had passed. Something made Robert feel glum and depressed, but he could not put his finger on it. He felt cheated that his night out had been taken away from him, stolen. Some time during the next hour, Pamela, his youngest sister, came around to see how he was. Carol had told Pamela that Robert sounded odd on the phone earlier that evening, and she wanted to make sure he was all right.

Under hypnosis we took him back to the clearing and suggested he might like to explore it, but there was something holding him back.

> I shouldn't go to the right. Get the feeling it's none of my business. It's awful dark there. I don't like to think of myself being frightened of the dark. If I go round that corner I'll see something ... I'll see somebody. It's those lights, they drew me out like a lighthouse ...

When we pressed Robert to go and look, he began breathing heavily. For the moment at least, there was an impenetrable block stopping further recollection.

The morning after the experience, Boxing Day, there was a knock at the door. It was one of Robert's neighbours, Diane, who wondered if he might want to join her for a celebration drink. But when she saw Robert's face she knew something was wrong. He told her about the strange lights coming down through the trees, and asked Diane if she would accompany him outside to examine the site. She agreed. Robert pulled on his jacket.

They were astounded to discover that the tall, rough weeds in the clearing were partially flattened in an elliptical pattern. More than this, there was a black, sticky substance adhering to the long stems. Nine months later, when the case came to the attention of Alicia Leigh, there was no trace of this substance. However, there was still evidence of damage to the area. Indeed, the weed growth seemed to be stunted. This was evident in a photograph she took. Alicia also discovered heat damage to three nearby trees.

Investigation

Plant, soil samples and damaged bark were collected. I arranged for laboratory analysis of the material at a local university. When the results were ready, Alicia and I went to discuss them with the department head. We learned that there was a huge discrepancy between the mineral oil content inside the affected area compared with a control sample from outside. The former contained 640 milligrams per kilogram of soil and the latter a mere sixty – a drop of over 90 per cent. What the significance of this might be is hard to see. A lack of time and money to carry out further analyses prevented us from pursuing the matter. It was concluded by the scientists that the fire damage to the tree bark was caused by an intense source of heat.

Alicia contacted the local taxi firm to see if they could verify that Robert had booked them that night. They were unable to provide Alicia with details, as such information was only available to the police. However, they did confirm that they had recorded a 'No show' on December 25. That meant that a taxi arrived to pick up a fare, but no one was at the address. Tony Eccles spoke to Air Traffic Control at Manchester International Airport, who stated there were no flights in the vicinity around the time that Robert first saw the strange lights.

Balls Of Light

During the interview and hypnosis sessions, Robert told us that he was not 'surprised' by the Christmas Day encounter. He felt it was connected with several childhood incidents which involved other members of his family.

Both Robert's brother and sister Pamela were plagued with lights. Pamela described small balls of light in her bedroom, a phenomenon that a number of UFO abductees have recounted. Robert's mother remembers seeing strange lights outside her window 'so close they scared me'. 'They were,' she said, red, blue and green, 'like Christmas lights.' She lay paralysed watching the lights, then remembers nothing else.

Both Mary Everett and Mike Sacks described small balls of light invading their rooms at night. After her UFO sighting and abduction Mary told me: 'The orange ball came that night. I was in bed and it came from my toes upwards. It didn't touch me, but floated just above my body, then travelled down again and disappeared.' When Mike Sacks was eleven or twelve he climbed out of bed one morning to see a green ball floating near the bedroom window. He felt as if it was probing his mind. Suddenly, the spell broke and he made a lunge for the ball. It vanished.

A Family Affair

During one of the hypnosis sessions Robert found himself at the mouth of a tunnel. He was about five or six years old, a little boy wearing a striped T-shirt, shorts and leather sandals. It began with him standing in the long grass of an idyll amongst trees heaving with pink and white blossom.

'I feel,' he said, 'that this image is blotting out something. I keep visualising a tunnel, a passageway, somewhere dark. It's big enough to stand in. I seem to be looking into it. It's grey, unnatural, as if it's been constructed. I associate danger with this tunnel. Don't want to go down there ...'

It was around 1969. Robert jumps from the tunnel episode to focus on the American moon landing, saying: 'The white suits of the astronauts look so clean, so sterile. I'm looking at the black visor. It reminds me of black liquid, a big eye, a pupil, shiny. I can imagine putting my finger in it and feeling it squelch back. The visor reminded me of something I have seen ...'

One of the incidents that plays on Robert's mind involves a shared UFO sighting. He was outside at the front of the family house in Whitefield with his little brother and sisters, as he explained under hypnosis. 'We were playing. Somebody's got some skipping ropes. There was Jacqui: she's wearing a little white jumper. There's Carol wearing a turquoise dress, and Daniel and I are wearing waistcoats. I can see the houses across the way.'

There was a friend with them, too. The boy's father bought them all ice creams from a van. They were running around playing as the light started to fade when suddenly a feeling of serenity stole over them. Robert looked up at the sky, then at the others who were also staring sky-wards. Something was up there ... But when we tried to obtain details from Robert we hit a dead end.

This is where I feel a little sad. We all feel sad because we were having such a good time. There's a block there. Something's happened and it's been kind of taken away. We all feel sad because we were having a good time playing. We're looking up and the sky is blue, but I'm having a hard time getting through the sky. It's like there's something there that's camouflaged. Looking up at that sky made you forget things ...

The 'blue sky' was really a mental screen imposed on him to hide what they saw that day. We worked with Robert until he felt ready to reveal what he saw.

It's ... I can't see it fully. I can see the tip. Triangular. Something ... I'm trying to understand why it's no big surprise ... It's like a big lump of grey metal in the sky. Just see the tip of it. It's just hanging there ... It's so dull and ugly, you know how you get battleship grey? It's like that, but so bloody ugly to look at.

We asked him what it reminded him of.

Something out of the Army or Air Force. But it's too big. It's like machinery, pistons, like cogs and very, very loud. I'm thinking, whoever's in there, how can they work with that noise? It's really loud, like a factory noise. It seems to be everywhere, like an air raid siren. It made me feel panicky, as if something was coming.

We wanted to know if his brother and sisters were showing any fear at seeing the object.

No. It's like if you went to a carnival, a fair ground, and saw the Big Wheel. You're looking up at it, and it's a massive thing. It's good to look at.

More than anything it was the feeling that affected them the most. It descended over them, wrapping and hugging them tight until they hurt, filling them with awe. Robert explained to me how he felt.

Despite the fact that he is not actively religious, this is the effect it had on him: 'It's all so serene, like looking up to heaven. There's a feeling that it's like the angels in the Bible, that they are looking after us. I think they're connected to God. I don't want to sound stupid, but I feel they're doing His work.'

Alerted by the noise, Robert's mother came outside to find out what was going on. We ask him to describe her reaction.

> It's different from ours. She's kind of amazed and scared because of the noise. It's so damn ugly …

Robert's siblings remember something of the incident, but not in any detail. However, Mrs Shawe was able to verify the account. 'I remember all the kids were playing at the front of the house when I heard a horrible sound, a loud buzzing,' she said. 'There was a corner of something sticking out of the clouds.'

Mrs Shawe brought the children inside and the noise abated. On a number of occasions, Robert impressed upon us his lack of surprise during the childhood encounter and the more recent Christmas Day experience. It was as if there were other encounters which had been deleted from his conscious memory. At times, however, the screen would lift a little.

> They make it difficult for you to remember,' he added. 'I get images of them. I keep thinking I'm seeing inside that thing. It's dull and ugly inside as well. It's grey and just like a big battleship. I can see things moving about in there. It reminds me of a beehive. They're forever busying themselves, darting around, going to one side then another, but I can't see any controls. They have to get you when you're young. I can see the yellowness of their skin.

We asked him why he felt so sad.

> It's like if your friends come to see you. You have a good time and then they go away. You feel sad because they've gone. You're having a good time, and it's not really fair because they shouldn't do that, not to children.

The other childhood incident that stuck in Robert's mind was an encounter with a being which had a direct bearing on the Christmas

Day incident. It took place when Robert was a few years older in the bedroom that he shared with his brother. The story emerged spontaneously during a hypnosis session. Although Daniel has no overt memory of it, it did strike a chord with him.

The boys slept in single beds side by side. That night, Robert fell asleep with his hand hanging over the edge of the bed. He awoke to find that something had hold of it. Before he could react, he was pulled onto the floor and something was trying to drag him beneath the bed. Robert fought fiercely and pulled away. Strangely, throughout this his brother remained asleep. The boy ran downstairs in his pyjamas to where his mum and dad were having a party. He found a quiet corner and hid. Not wanting to spoil the fun, he said nothing, sitting there, feeling guilty he had left Daniel in the room with that thing ...

On another occasion, Robert said he was woken by Daniel, who was pointing towards a being in the room. Daniel was standing in his little striped pyjamas, nodding his head as if in answer to something the being had said. Then he came over to Robert and told him the being wanted to speak to him now. However, Daniel has no overt recollection of this. Did the beings blot it from his memory?

> I'm in my bedroom. I can see it in the corner, beside the chest of drawers. The curtains are open, the moon's out and there's a shimmer of light coming through. It's dipping in and out of the shadows, but I can't see its legs. I don't want to be here. I'm looking down at the pattern on the bed spread, anywhere but over there, but I'm drawn towards it ... He's craning over me. He reminds me of when you go to the cemetery where they have those big statues of angels. They lean over you when you're small and you're looking up at them.
>
> I can't relate it to anything I've seen before. Its head is huge, as if it's too heavy for the neck. I can see its forehead, its big eyes, and parts of its mouth. I pulled back the blankets and got out of bed holding onto the bed rail. Its head's moving, coming forwards slightly, then going back into the shadows.'

The motion of the head was particularly bizarre, as Robert emphasised. '"Nodding" is the word I'm looking for or "bobbing". It reminds me of a float at the end of a fishing line, the way it bobs in the water.'

Robert said the being was hairless, and its skin a mustard colour, although the area around the cheek bones was brown. He 'knew', possibly from another, hidden encounter, that 'they're kind of gangly'.

The face looks like plasticine, rubbery, as if you could smear it. There's a rim or ridge around the eyes. The head looks like a dome and the mouth is just a heavy line. I don't think I can see a nose. The top lip is moving as if he's talking, but he's not talking. You can hear the words but, there's no sound from the mouth. He feels and you feel.

When asked what he was thinking, a small boy looking up at the thing, Robert answered: 'It doesn't come across as something that would do me any harm, but it's not very nice to look at. It's scary! They want us to be their friends.'

Robert described the lenses of its eyes as 'thick, that if you could touch them it would be like putting your finger in paint, or oil'.

Robert's attitude towards the being is ambivalent. As we have seen, this is a common reaction. He feels in some way it is 'angelic', yet it also frightens him. It has come, he believes, to fill him with good thoughts, to make him behave better towards others. This bedroom visitor, we subsequently discovered, was at the core of the Christmas Day encounter.

Down In The Woods
During further hypnosis sessions we attempted to pierce the barrier that was preventing Robert from telling us what else happened that night. It seemed that there was certainly more to the account. How else could we explain the missing time? When we asked what was holding him back, Robert replied: 'I'm not supposed to say. I could get into trouble. It might spoil things for the future, and I don't want to spoil things for my brothers and sisters.'

I decided to try an experiment used successfully by Professor John Mack. Mack is the former head of the Department of Psychiatry at the Cambridge Hospital, Harvard Medical School. Robert could not re-live the full experience under hypnosis because he was too afraid to turn the corner and walk into the clearing. But what if we could persuade him to do that by proxy? I told Robert to visualise a small robot which was under his control. Then I asked Robert to send the robot into the clearing to record what was happening. Finally, I requested that he should tell us what the robot had reported to him.

> There's silhouettes moving about in the woods, busying themselves, reminding me of bees. There's something in the clearing. It's not a tree, but it looks like a tree trunk, maybe the size of a double decker bus, maybe more. I'm not sure I'm supposed to see, I might get into trouble for this …

Robert suddenly tensed up.

> There's an image coming through, and it's … something's coming towards me … the sort of thing I saw as a kid … it's the same one! He's come forwards, and now he's standing there.

The first aspect that hit Robert was that the being now seemed small, but as a child he was looking up at him. This removed the fear Robert had felt all those years before. It half smiled at him and then communicated through his emotions. 'He never says anything,' Robert explained. 'You just feel it.'

We asked Robert how he was feeling.

> As if he's a long lost friend … Everything's going to be okay. I'm looking down on him now, because I'm bigger, and he's not scary. He's just saying "Everything's going to be fine", and he's telling me I've got to go back to the flat. It feels right to go back. It's like seeing a friend you've not seen for years, who's heard you're not doing too well, telling you not to worry, don't worry …

Robert was now able to give us a fuller description of the object.

> It's cylindrical, a column about the height of a double decker bus. The top of the structure is curved. I feel it's organic, leafy, twiggy and it looks mossy. I don't like to think I've touched it as it reminds me of being mucky. It's like wet bark with things like barnacles living on it.

What did he mean by 'mucky'?

> It reminds me of when I played out in the woods and came home full of muck. I'm with Daniel, Carole and Pamela in Jackson's Wood. We're laughing and shouting, playing in the falling leaves, feeling them crunching underfoot. We're saying that perhaps once there were bears and getting ourselves spooked. The woods aren't too bad a place as long as you're with someone …

Once again, Robert stood before the object, and under hypnosis, experienced a strange emotion. We asked him to try and put it into words.

> Imagine walking through the woods during day time and seeing the wind blowing through the branches of a tree. That tree really seems alive. If you visited the wood on another occasion when it's still and damp perhaps it's been raining and the trees seem dead, as if they are switched off. This object is definitely not a tree, but it has taken on that dead quality.

Robert believes that the entity responded to his state of mind that Christmas Day, and came to reassure him that everything would come right in his life.

> It was just before Christmas, paying out bills. My personal life wasn't up to much. Had a lot on my mind. Things were bad, then the lights came. They cheered me up so much. They were really beautiful.

We asked him to elaborate.

> You must know how it felt. When you're a child and you're not feeling very happy. Your mum and dad take you to a zoo or a fun fair and it cheers you up.

Robert sent out an SOS and the entity responded. His guardian angel. Yet the being's appearance and behaviour are far from angelic. The UFO entity looks like a hobgoblin and his tactics are not exactly friendly. Robert's comments on the relationship serve to emphasise this incongruity.

I get the impression they look after those with a good heart. They're connected with God, doing His work, servants of some kind. They want to help you emotionally by making you complete. All goodness comes from the heart, not the mind. If you think with the heart then you'll never go wrong. They look after their own.

The fear element of the relationship comes through in these comments:

They're very much in control. Authoritarian is too strong a word, but he's in control. I feel resentment towards it. It makes me angry.

Indeed, on several occasions during hypnosis, Robert would take refuge when confronted with this fear in an idyll which he has created in his mind. In the midst of his fear, he would transport himself to a place of green fields, hills and trees heavy with summer blossom. 'It's sunny,' he said on one of his visits, 'and it's funny because I don't seem to have a care in the world. It's a happy place to be, and there's nobody else there to bother or frighten you.'

Often, abduction imagary surfaces through dreams. Robert told us of a recurring dream in which he was taken to a 'reception' by one of his uncles. The room was white and clinical looking. There was a window with blinds. Magazines were strewn across a table. Uncle Stan was sitting on an orange plastic chair with black iron legs. He was wearing sun-glasses with black, impenetrable lenses. Robert was waiting for something to happen.

There's a man talking to me. He's unshaven and his hair is untidy. He looks the sort of guy who wouldn't bother too much about buying a shirt. I got the impression that he was drunk because he wasn't making any sense.

He was angry about something, and was trying to get something through to me. But I found him intimidating, yet I felt I knew the man. He reminded me of my mother's other brother who had died, but this man was far too unkempt. I'd like to know what he was trying to tell me.

In the dream Robert felt an impression of what lay beyond the reception area in a room.

> A totally blinding white, clinical environment: clean, pure, sterile. It's a lonely place and gives me a creepy feeling because there's nothing to touch in that place.

It would be an easy option to confine close encounter and abduction cases to the filing cabinets of psychiatrists. But I know from more than twenty years of research and investigation that no matter how bizarre they seem, these experiences represent a very real facet of alien activity. It is a highly complex phenomenon that manifests in our reality and interacts with percipients on a level tailor-made to their understanding. The beings' mind control techniques make black seem white, and blank out those incidents, or segments of incidents, which it does not want reported. What Robert described that Christmas night was in essence a flying Christmas tree, with lights in a zigzag pattern that put those on his own tree to shame.

'It's a beautiful sight,' Robert told us. 'It makes me feel good.'

Robert explained the relationship between the beings and ourselves in this way:

> You know when you see a cute little boy or little girl, and you buy them a lolly pop, or you put your arm around them: you know how people are with little kids? That's how they look upon us. They find us very interesting.

The behaviour of angels, or the tactics of child molesters? At one point Robert explained how the being's eyes were 'very deep. You could get lost in them. They're like fathomless wells. Windows of the soul.'

What sort of soul has black eyes, I wondered?

9

Within You Without You

Robert Shawe's experiences bring us full circle. In them there are some very powerful clues to the real nature of the alien phenomenon. He said about the object in the clearing:

> It's not a tree, but it looks like a tree trunk. The top of the structure is curved. I feel it's organic, leafy, twiggy and it looks mossy. I don't like to think I've touched it. It reminds me of being mucky. It's like wet bark with things like barnacles living on it.

Robert compares it to a tree in winter time on a still, damp day:

> This object is definitely not a tree, but it has taken on that dead quality.

The entities – perhaps for their amusement – like to drop in these clues. Or are they mocking us? When Mary Everett stood on her doorstep watching the UFO, she later told me, 'I had a feeling it had come from the Earth.' Despite this and the overwhelming evidence in this book, blind believers still make fools of themselves by insisting that UFOs are space ships and that the beings are extraterrestrials from other planets. The sceptics and debunkers unwittingly join in the game by attacking the proponents of the extraterrestrial hypothesis because they cannot handle the truth.

So what exactly are we dealing with? We are faced with an invasive force that can operate on many levels. It is as much psychological as physical, working through consciousness as well as through the tactile material world. The intelligences behind the UFO phenomenon can juggle matter like we can conjure up drinks in a cocktail shaker. They create customised 'craft' that are able to appear as balls of light or nuts and bolts machines that could have been manufactured on an assembly line. These UFOs may not be vehicles at all, but portals between their world and ours – 'doorways' that can manifest in outer space, the atmosphere or in a woodland glade.

Vallee reminds us of 'Magonia', the name given to the land of the fairies. He writes: 'Magonia constitutes a sort of parallel universe which co-exists with our own. It is made visible and tangible only to selected people, and the doors that lead through it are tangential points, known only to the elves and a few of their initiates.'

When forestry worker Bob Taylor had a close encounter experience in November 1979 his observations included something which was very telling.

Bob walked into a clearing in woods near Livingston, Scotland, and came across a circular object. The middle-aged man was seriously assaulted during his encounter. The police cordoned off the area and carried out an investigation. When I asked Bob to describe the object, he said that although it looked solid, at times parts of it faded in and out so he could see bushes and trees through it. This was not a 'flying' object at all, but an intruder from another dimension. They can operate in the physical world and be filmed, photographed and tracked on radar, then disappear in a puff of smoke.

Do the aliens 'wear' bodies as Whitley Strieber suggests? Are biological entities created which the beings then operate like ghosts in a machine? This would explain the stiff, robotic movement of the entities described by many witnesses, including Ken Edwards.

But the beings can also penetrate the inner space of the mind. They walk into our dreams and affect our thoughts, create fear and model our behaviour. Many alien encounters have a dream-like quality to them, but patently they are more than just dreams.

It is worth considering at this point that there might not be any aliens …

Whitley Strieber said that the beings were insect-like and acted as if they had a job to do. Both Philip Spencer and Robert Shawe compared the aliens' behaviour to that of bees. 'It reminds me of a beehive,' Shawe said, describing the UFO. 'The creatures seemed part of a team,' Spencer told me. 'They weren't acting as individuals, but more like bees, as if they were doing what they were programmed to do.'

These observations echo those of countless other abductees and close encounter percipients. Is there a central alien intelligence that uses biological entities to carry out its will? It sounds like science fiction, but science fiction is based on fact, and fiction makes a habit of coming true … If nothing else, the UFO phenomenon teaches us that the boundaries between fantasy and reality are blurred – if they exist at all. 'Reality' is often what the majority of people agree it is at a particular point in time.

Sceptics often say, 'It's just imagination.' Of course, they are right. Imagination shapes our world. Without imagination nothing would ever change, either on a personal or societal level. Imagination is a powerful mental faculty for making sense of events around us. It is a decoder for interpreting encounters with other-world beings. Imagination is what perhaps makes us different from the other animals. That, and a bit of tinkering.

Charles Fort, a sceptic of religious and scientific institutions, once said, 'I think we are property.' After almost twenty-five years' study and investigation of UFO-related experiences, I think Fort might be right. The evidence suggests to me that a very long time ago something adopted us as its property and has been in control ever since. Humans are really nothing more than genetically modified animals.

Did an alien intelligence take a primitive ape and then genetically modify it at the beginning of a programme of experimentation that continues to this day? We are the only animal that kicks against the forces of nature and destroys its environment. As a species we have become a cancer on the Earth. Is that *natural*?

Is the Earth a nature reserve? Are the aliens the park-keepers who trap us and carry out medical procedures? Do they sometimes test us against new diseases, use genetic material to create hybrids, give us cancers and introduce other fatal illnesses into society? Would a wild rabbit have any more understanding of the being who darts it for testing in a laboratory than we have of the UFO intelligences who abuse members of the human species? Does the rat dropped into a maze have any idea at all of why he is there? If not, then why should we? It is often an uphill struggle trying to make sense of something which is so 'alien'.

Talking about his 'visitors', Whitley Strieber told ufologist Michael Miley, 'They are what the force of evolution looks like to a conscious mind.' I think Strieber is partially right. The aliens certainly represent a force of change, but it is brought about through control. They are a force of control more than a force of evolution.

They control our evolution, our religious and cultural beliefs, our environment, and our intellectual and personal freedom. The 'aliens' can come and go with impunity. We are powerless to do anything about it. They can take people at will, and enter our dreams as easily as they invade our air space. They can mock us and hurt us, but they are not really cruel – just indifferent.

Our destiny is in their hands.

References

Much of the material contained in this book is the result of my own investigation and research into the UFO phenomenon. However, a title of this nature requires reference to some of my previous works, and that of others who have specialised in certain areas of the UFO subject. Below are listed the main sources of reference.

1: Exposing the Big Lie

Blumrich, Josef *The Spaceships of Ezekiel* (Bantam 1974)

Bord, Janet *Fairies* (Michael O'Mara 1997)

Evans & Spencer, Hilary & John (Editors) *UFOs 1947 – 1987* (Fortean Tomes 1987)

Hancock, Graham *Fingerprints of the Gods* (Mandarin 1996)

Hough & Kalman, Peter & Moyshe *The Truth About Alien Abductions* (Blandford 1997)

Hough & Randles, Peter & Jenny *Looking For The Aliens* (Blandford 1992)

Lafferty & Rowe, Peter & Julian *The Hutchinson Dictionary of Science* (Helicon 1993)

Leslie & Adamski, Desmond & George *Flying Saucers Have Landed* (Werner Laurie 1954)

Spencer & Evans, John & Hilary (Editors) *Phenomenon* (Futura 1988)

Story, Ronald *The Space Gods Revealed* (New English Library 1977)

Temple, K. G., Robert *The Sirius Mystery* (Futura 1976/Century 1998)

Wentz, W. Y. Evans *The Fairy-Faith In Celtic Countries* (Copyright 1911 Colin Smythe 1977)

Vallee, Jacques *Passport To Magonia* (Neville Spearman 1970)

Vallee, Jacques *Dimensions* (Souvenir 1988)

The Bible (Collins 1952)

2: The Development of Alien Activity

Good, Timothy *Above Top Secret* (Sidgwick & Jackson 1987)

Hough & Randles, Peter & Jenny *The Complete Book of UFOs* (Piatkus 1994, 1997)

Redfern, Nicholas *The FBI Files* (Simon & Schuster 1998)

'The Mini People' by Peter Hough *The Unknown* May 1986

3: The Secret Inquiry in America

Good, Timothy *Above Top Secret* (Sidgwick & Jackson 1987)

Hough & Randles, Peter & Jenny *Looking For The Aliens* (Blandford 1992)

Hough & Randles, Peter & Jenny *The Complete Book of UFOs* (Piatkus 1994, 1997)

Randles, Jenny *The UFO Conspiracy* (Blandford 1987)

Redfern, Nicholas *A Covert Agenda* (Simon & Schuster 1997)

Redfern, Nicholas *The FBI Files* (Simon & Schuster 1998)

4: The Secret Inquiry in Britain

Good, Timothy *Above Top Secret* (Sidgwick & Jackson 1987)

Hough & Randles, Peter & Jenny *The Complete Book of UFOs* (Piatkus 1994, 1997)

Randles, Jenny *The UFO Conspiracy* (Blandford 1987)

Redfern, Nicholas *A Covert Agenda* (Simon & Schuster 1997)

5: The Secret Inquiry Elsewhere

Bray, Arthur *The UFO Connection* (Jupiter Publishing 1979)

Good, Timothy *Above Top Secret* (Sidgwick & Jackson 1987)

Hough & Randles, Peter & Jenny *Looking For The Aliens* (Blandford 1992)

Hough & Randles, Peter & Jenny *The Complete Book of UFOs* (Piatkus 1994, 1997)

Randles, Jenny *The UFO Conspiracy* (Blandford 1987)

Redfern, Nicholas *A Covert Agenda* (Simon & Schuster 1997)

6: A Dangerous Liaison

Bray, Arthur *The UFO Connection* (Jupiter Publishing 1979)

Hough & Kalman, Peter & Moyshe *The Truth About Alien Abductions* (Blandford 1997)

Hough & Randles, Peter & Jenny *The Complete Book of UFOs* (Piatkus 1994, 1997)

Randles & Hough, Jenny & Peter *Encyclopedia Of The Unexplained* (Michael O'Mara 1995)

Randles & Hough, Jenny & Peter *Death By Supernatural Causes?* (Grafton 1987)

Vallee, Jacques *Dimensions* (Souvenir Press 1988)

'Down On The Farm' by David Cayton *UFO Magazine* (Jan/Feb 1999)

'Witness Burned By Passing UFO' by Tony Green *Flying Saucer Review* (Vol 26, No 5)

7: Control Freaks

Randles, Jenny *The Pennine UFO Mystery* (Granada 1983)

Randles & Warrington, Jenny & Peter *Science and the UFOs* (Basil Blackwell 1985)

8: Dark Angel

'What Kind Of Soul Has Black Eyes?' by Peter Hough *FATE* (September 1998, Vol 51, No 9)

9: Within You Without You

Hough & Kalman, Peter & Moyshe *The Truth About Alien Abductions* (Blandford 1997)

Randles & Hough, Jenny & Peter *Strange But True?* (Piatkus 1994)

Vallee, Jacques *Dimensions* (Souvenir 1988)

'What Kind Of Soul Has Black Eyes?' by Peter Hough *FATE* (September 1998, Vol 51, No 9)

Index